loving the loveless

loving the loveless

an animal rescuer's stories of love, courage, and hope

taken from the reluctant rescuer blog

www.thereluctantrescuer.com

Acknowledgements

I would like to acknowledge the unlimited help and support of Pat Tobin, who made my dream of a sanctuary for abused animals a reality. Hilltop Sanctuary is a special place: there is a special togetherness here that is formed from the same difficult beginning in life the rescues share. Together they heal and together they live the lives they deserve. We will never be able to change where they came from or their terrible experiences, but we are privileged to create a very different ending for them.

I would also like to acknowledge my family and friends who are a constant source of support. I am sure my parents imagined a very different path for me, and I hope the path that found me has not disappointed them. My father invested a lot in my education, and I probably have not put my academic ability to full use or realised career ambitions they would have had for me. However, my ability to navigate the complex rescue world, to engage with diverse people, and build a rapport, is a testament perhaps to everything that went into my upbringing.

To all the animal rescuers, advocates and animal lovers, please continue the good fight: to be their voice, to fight for their rights as outlined in animal welfare legislation, and to love them more to make up for those who neglect or abuse them. One day it will change – that day is coming.

Disclaimer

This is a book containing posts from The Reluctant Rescuer Blog. The posts are usually written late in the night or early in the morning. The thoughts are automatic, and the sentiment is heartfelt. The conveying words are often raw and unpolished. If you are unable for bad grammar or lack of punctuation, please look away now! In my world, there is so little room for editing which I regret. Many posts were put together through teary eyes and exhaustion. My sole aim is always to give a voice to the voiceless in my posts and to keep loving the loveless.

To my mother, Anne, who thought me
all I need to know about compassion.
I want to acknowledge all the animals that inspire these
posts. I dedicate it to those who never made
it 'home'. A home that would have cared for them, and a
home that would have been there for them as they took
their last breath in this world.

Introduction

This book documents my journey as a rescuer and feeder over the last few years. It is only when I read the posts in book format that I am struck by some of the 'out of character' things I have done for animals in need, and I am left with the realisation that I'm not sure if I could do what my past-self has done: I'm not sure I am as brave as I once was but perhaps it was a blind bravery. Now that my 'eyes are wide open' I see everything I chose not to see that perhaps would have made me turn my back many times. But I did what I did for the love of them: the animals that needed me to act, to be the person to do something. There's a part of me that sometimes I do not recognise: the part that risked so much so I would not be another person to let them down. I also faced many of my fears to do so; I never overcame them.

In an age where animal cruelty is very much part of our world, where some humans feel an entitlement to own without providing care, where animals are used for a negative need fulfilment, or where they are simply abused as an outlet for some people's ills, the stories here serve to remind us: where they are does not always mean that they must stay there. Just because they are unloved does not mean they have to remain so. We all can be part of creating new endings.

Animals gave me a life purpose that not just filled a void but pushed what I believed to be important aside: the trivia that I once labelled as significant. Trivia that often stole my peace of mind.

The animals that crossed my path may have been loveless, but they were and are very capable of showing endless love. It is a great pity that there are owners out there who will never show loving kindness or basic care to their animals. They will never experience the unconditional love that animals innately have for the person in their lives.

I am no one special, just one person who happened to cross paths with one pony, who was akin to an equine whistle-blower. It was her frail, aching, starved body tied to a steel barrier that made me open my eyes to all the others suffering on roads I travelled most days. I simply never saw them until I saw her. She became the hero of so many that came after her. It is because of her that I ended up rescuing so many horses; it's because of her so many left this world knowing love and not dying alone.

Animals are life's greatest companions, family members, and teachers. Their greatness should be matched with deserving protection when people neglect or abuse them. No one in your life will love you constantly and consistently the way an animal does.

once upon a time

The story that was told before it began . . .

Over a decade ago, a friend of mine asked me to go with her to a fortune teller – one that charged a substantial amount of money, which in some way gave her an elevated credibility above many other tellers out there. Dragging my heels, I went, and left with much regret that evening thinking 'what I could have done with the cash'. My card reading became the 'joke story' I shared with many over the years that followed, until my life began to mimic the cards: their images and their stories.

The reading lasted an hour in a smoke-filled room with all sorts of colourful shrines to her faith overlooking us. My future forecast had 'nothing to do with me', I politely protested, after she had turned over the cards I had picked with intention from her shuffled pile, and she read them for me. Then cupping my hands facing up, she read the textless lines with both pity and frustration: she seemed to see much of the sameness. Her tone was matter of fact as she repeated what she already had seen from the cards, whilst telling her Mammy what she didn't want for dinner when asked. She sighed many times as her cigarette smouldered away,

1

balanced on the tip of her coloured red lips. I even remember a polite pitiful apology. She knew what she saw, and she told me her cards did not lie. I took none of it seriously. My future plans had nothing to do with what she forecast. Besides, I knew I didn't want to stay working in a secondary school. That was a certainty.

But, from start to finish, horses and helping were the common theme of the cards before me. I was there (she pointed again and again!) leading them out of dark valleys and towards a better life. I was there holding a lantern guiding them, and they were following me. I laughed as I told her that the last time I was on a horse, he threw me off, and that is where I parted ways with equines. His name was Guinness and I was 16 years old. I only went riding on a weekly basis to keep another friend happy.

She wished me well with the horses as I paid her. 'But there are no horses . . .' I half-smiled, as she politely led me towards her front door. She had warned my friend to mind me too which didn't go down well. Her predictions for me had invaded her reading time.

... and here I am, years later, the reluctant rescuer and feeder. It all started when driving my pride and joy, a little baby blue convertible, one bright Spring day. Thinking life was good, my gaze was diverted to *her*. 'Her' being a pony tied up on an embankment at the side of the road. I didn't want to see her: I was going shopping. But I indicated and pulled in. Surveying the steep walk ahead of me if I was to check her out, I looked at my shoes, and then I looked at her staring down at me. With one step forward and a few backwards, I eventually reached her by grabbing onto newly planted trees up to her. Yes, we had a moment that I cannot put into words, and without thinking, I said out loud, 'you are not staying here! I am getting you out of here. I promise you!'

She was tied inside steel barriers that ran along each side of an access road to farmland. The ground beneath ploughed from her pacing up and down as far as her four-foot, blue, fraying rope would allow her. The guilt of having nothing to give her probably imprinted on me, that now my car is never without food for a horse or any animal. So, I told her, I would be back, and as I literally slid back down to my car, I was faced with a few puzzled faces as I said 'goodbye' to a small, coloured, tethered pony.

'What are you doing up there with my pony?' asked one of them gruffly. I just made barely audible apologetic sounds as I slid passed their circle to get back into my car. But my quick exit didn't materialise – thanks to a bad battery and leaving hazard lights on. And so began a conversation about a pony that was theirs, and I crawled into the issue of where she was tied and its suitability. They saw nothing wrong with the rope that now had formed an inexplicable connection between me and her. As we talked, she started to whinny. They seemed amused at her calling. 'Isn't she calling ye?' I asked. They looked at each other. 'She must be happy to see ye,' I added. They found that even more amusing as a tattooed hand reached out for my keys, and I surrendered them without either of us saying a word.

I learned from the start the importance of keeping in with

certain owner because sometimes despite all the reporting and phoning and quoting animal welfare legislation to authorities, a horse's life is left in a rescuer's hands and a deal will be have to be made between you and the owners. Sometimes I got lucky with a surrender after much pestering, and sometimes the only lifeline I could throw a horse dying, was money in the hands of her owner.

'Sure, we'll try get her going for ya,' he told me as he jumped into my car. I watched my dead car being pushed; she stayed in my sight down the by-pass with the driver door swinging open. It didn't take long for them to give up. The sloping road helped them get further than they should have. There was a wave to say, 'no luck' and they walked away from my car. One of them shouted back and I just laughed – no clue as to what he just said. But he knew I hadn't heard him. He shouted again, 'her name is Mini'. Time showed me he was probably the best owner out of a bad lot. It was his phone I would ring in the future to try reach other owners. He was probably the only owner over time that I could actually give out to and get away with it. Many others warned me in different ways to stay silent 'or else'.

That day, I looked up to my new friend with big brown eyes and a shaggy coat. 'Hello, Mini,' I smiled.

Years later, I can tell you, those cards did not lie. I've been and continue to be in many testing 'valleys', but I've felt the relief and exhilaration of the peaks: horses rescued who go on to the most amazing homes where often they are not recognisable from their rescue day. Seeing a horse run towards a gate knowing 'his/her rescue day has come' when transport arrives, draws both tears and smiles. Rescue days are like tattoos: they stay with you forever. Seeing horses that will never be rescued run to a gate when they see you pulling up with food is like the fairy tale that will never have the generic happy ending. Not being able to take them is heart-breaking. Not being able to end their suffering hurts at times. I never remember how many I have saved; I remember the ones I didn't with dreadful ease. It is so difficult to love an animal that will never be yours. Just as much as it is to love a person, I guess.

There is one piece to her fortune telling that I hope will never come true, but time will reveal that. For now, what remains constant is them: beautiful horses let down terribly by people called 'owners' or others who cross their paths.

There are these tiny pockets of doubt that appear when I am away from them. In those bubbles are perfect, vivid reminders of 'the before'. Yes, I want to give up and run – run back to my other life, the life that I look back on like a tourist now. What remains of it is a wardrobe of glittering and glamorous clothes far removed from wet gear and boots. There are stacks of books I once looked forward to reading and piles of A4 paper with 'the beginnings' of new books I planned to write. What also remains of my previous life are framed photos hanging on walls of a stranger that shares my name but not my life now. It is still nice to reminisce though. Everything was so different back then, But, when I'm with them, I want to be nowhere else. I feel complete.

The parts that make us fragmented but whole

January 2018

We really are a sum of parts! At any one time we can love and hate at the same time! It feels like a fight within: the part that wins is the part we feed, many would say.

Rescue life accentuates these parts: I often feel a constant tug of war within. The part of me that is too proud to ask for help is overpowered by the part that is desperate for help for an animal in need. The part of me that loves the animals I feed, hates the type of owner who has brought me here. It is a type of love desperate to make things better that keeps me coming back: the love and care for an animal who might never be mine! But I always hope – hope that one day they will know another life. I never say never until the horse is dead or sold on. I have heard the word 'No' many times but in the rescue world words are often cheap. Often 'No' quickly changes to 'how much will you give for her?' to 'take her out of the field cos I don't want to be looking at a dead horse in the morning!'

When I first started rescuing and feeding hungry horses, I told few, and I asked for no help! How can people help when you never ask? However, the proud part of me is silenced by a desperate need for donations or the desperate need for transport or rescue space. I think I'm now without any pride; it has been starved! What struck me about rescues is this: you may have to ask for help once or twice but after that 'Can you help?' is quickly replaced with 'Do you need any help?' Busy rescues like My Lovely Horse, Charlie's, Hungry Horse Outside, Putting in the Magic and Forgotten Horses Ireland, along with some great foster homes always seem to have a place for 'just one more!'. I'm forever in debt to them for taking pigs and ponies off me. The part of me that was initially too proud to ask has no place in rescue!

Rescuers are constantly connected by lives saved and lives lost. The sense of togetherness sometimes makes me feel less alone. And that is a part I struggled with greatly in the past and still at times now: the loneliness of rescue. Especially on cold frosty nights with a florescent moon illuminating everything around you like a spotlight, and as you feed, this field stage suddenly draws you in. The bitter air draws animated bubbles with the words you speak to the animals. All that exists is you and them. Yes, it's a lonely time of night when you say your goodbyes, and you pass sleeping houses where people are cuddled up and safe.

So much has happened this week already! The worry of one horse is quickly replaced by the other. There are many requests for help. Some don't seem to realise that I am no different to them: I am just this ordinary person who has begun to love and care too much. But it is the 'too much' part that fuels my rescue work and drive. So, when those closest to me give out about caring too much or getting so upset or angry, I realise the day I stop is the day I will stop rescuing.

There is another part of me that craves to be anonymous and just carry on as if I am working behind closed curtains. But no real change comes from silence. Authorities will never act or start doing their job consistently and implementing the welfare legislation unless rescuers and advocates keep highlighting and fighting for these animals. Because their suffering is real. So just pottering away with a 'nothing to see here' will change nothing in the long-term.

In an effort to protect my own privacy, I used to give out different names to different owners. That 'not very well thought out plan' came apart the other day when three different horse owners stood chatting to me! All three called me variations of my own name until one said: 'Jesus, you've a name on all the horses and you've many names on yourself!'

Again, the part of me that wants to scream 'feed your horses' never gets heard as the part of me that wants to build bridges and to feed their horses pleads for silence! This forced silence had me leading a pony I feed out of her lane to a yard, where I watched her getting new shoes put on; I also watched her fear build and her breathing escalate. They cannot catch her so the only way they would do it is to instil fear and exhaustion by running her until she gives up. I wanted to save her from that. The part of me that loves her but hates the sulky waiting for her tries to calm her, talk to her, and tries to block out the sounds of rasps and hammers falling to the ground. The part of me that felt I betrayed her won on this occasion. I cried all the way home.

A young traveller boy once asked me, 'do I only feed horses I like?' His fear is I won't like his next horse and therefore I won't feed her. So that started us onto talking about me helping him feed her. Time will tell how productive that conversation was. I was relieved to see how kind he could be with one mare I asked him to help me feed. What initially brought me to his address was a pony lodged between two concrete bollards. Nobody came to help but rescuers. It was another rescue group that sent me out to help after twelve calls to the guards and the department proved futile. That pony is now very well and very happy with FHI. In one way it was a blessing in disguise as two Shetlands here also needed rescuing, and I am happy to say that the those two smallies who lived on concrete are now with Lorraine in a beautiful green field with a stable. And back to my conversation with my little helper! He pointed out to me, 'Catriona, the horses all look at you when you're here! Is it cos you are nice to them?' I replied, 'Yes, and because I feed them too!' He thought about what I was saying before he responded, 'they look at me the same way!'

This site is difficult to drive into, and as I park, I have to breathe deeply and talk myself into getting out, unloading, and then lifting hay and bottles of water to the many horses here – some loose and some tethered. It seems to be only the kids here who have an interest in them, but kids do not have the means to feed them or the knowledge to care properly. The older men are often congregated around one of the homes, but they never offer help – maybe they don't know how to.

Today my new rescue friend drove me around to feed the horses along the motorway! I told him 'I better get the most of you before you disappear!' He tells me he is 'in it for the long haul!' My prayers will start now!! I can't tell you what it's like to have somebody who can lift a bale of hay like they are lifting a pillow! To feed the three donkeys (latest to the feeding programme) requires fence jumping and wading through muck to get to them. I walked with ease today! No, it wasn't easy to hear the words 'that's poison' when my friend looked at what their owner left for them. Sometimes I really want to be wrong! I want them to be OK and I want to hear the words, 'you've nothing to worry about' but most of the time there is so much to worry about! The wealthy owner in this case is neglecting his animals! The part that hates this behaviour can take over and so I had a heated phone conversation with a welfare inspector. The agreement was: the owner would leave hay and it was made over two weeks ago! Still no hay! Many people think it is a case of just ringing a welfare number and all will be well. Yes, I once was naïve enough to believe that too. In ten years, no one paid to help has ever helped an animal I reported. The odd notice was stuck up on gates, but the weather made sure they never lasted. I must add this important point: feeding hungry horses does not let any owner off the hook. They let themselves off! The fact is: this type of owner does not care whether their horses are hungry or not. Their attitude is 'there are lots where they came from'. With no deterrents or enforced requirements for horse ownership – they keep adding to their stock. And one authorised officer told me, feeding a horse will not get in the way of them being seized once they know the owner is not feeding them. He still didn't seize a mare called Nollaig after he told me she can pick around the trees. The trees had just moss on them, I pleaded. He just walked back into his van.

I want to remember Hutch tonight, the twelve-year-old dog killed in Mountrath. His family's world is now changed forever as they have lost a family member in the cruellest way possible. I also want to remember the pony in Ennis we couldn't find in a flooded field, only to learn when we left the field that she had died. She died alone, with no access to feed and in water. I cried as I drove away with a bag of hay meant for her.

Yes, I struggle with the parts of me that feel complete hatred for the people who cause so much suffering and yet I wonder did they suffer terribly at some stage in their lives? In the case of Hutch, I worry for the sadistic behaviour these people are capable of. Part of me feels sorry for the part of them that must be so deprived of love, care, and compassion that they could do this. Yet, part of me wants them to feel the pain they caused the beautiful and noble Hutch.

To end on a lighter note, I was really hungry earlier and given my mucky attire, I went with my friend to the restaurant in the mart. I was relieved I couldn't hear any of the cow calls that

11

can be upsetting for some of us. Anyway, here were hard working men lined up in their wellies. I fitted right in until I asked the girl behind the counter 'was there anything for vegetarians?' I answered my own question when there was a sudden silence in the cafeteria style room after she repeated much louder my enquiry! 'Hardly in a mart,' I laughed awkwardly. She said nothing but smiled and I got a plate of veg. And then it was off to collect a round bale of donated haylage and bring it down the by-pass to fork some into Erin, Bella, Nollaig, Holly, and Finn. Tomorrow it's the motorway horses and more feeding around town. It's the part of me that can never give up on them that I'm feeding for now!

Fifty Shades of Hay

February 2018

I remember the first year of equine rescue and feeding – on long trips with fellow rescuers like Joe from Charlie's – I would ask with much frustration and bemusement, 'how did it come to this?' 'This' being a life far removed from what I planned! Poor Joe would be hit with the hungry and probably selfish question many times when moving horses, and I know inside he was probably laughing: I was just beginning on the road where he worked tirelessly for many decades. He must have thought 'she won't last the year!' Joe never answered me because he knew it was something I had to answer for myself. 'How did it come to this?' Well, I stopped asking after the first year: I guess it became like 'leaves to trees': natural, and part of life: beginnings and endings. Longing to see them and hating the chaos my life existed in. The love and hate colliding again and again. One of the shades of rescue.

My car broke down yesterday with 4 of my rescue dogs inside. Many people tried to help as the dogs tried to do what they thought was their 'job': protect me and the car! My friend Linda and Kevin tried to jump-start it, but it was more complex than a dead battery. So, a lovely but 'didn't want to be there' AA man arrived. First, he wouldn't get into the car with the dogs and I could see from his eyes, his look of 'what the hell?' as he saw the dogs on thrones of hay or nuts, and that very memorable smell of haylage came to meet him as I rolled down the window to talk to him when he first arrived. Another shade of rescue: being judged! He didn't spend long trying to figure out the problem, and the car with the four dogs within were towed away as I sat upfront! It had been a long time since I had asked the question but this time I did it silently.

I began the calls for help to do the feeding rounds. Otherwise I would expect the horses around Ennis to arrive at my door to question the delay with breakfast! Breakfast I'm afraid became supper! The guilt: another shade of rescue. They would have been standing at the gates waiting. Nollaig, a dark lonely mare was probably there all day – where I found her last night! There is very little around the trees to sustain her which was deemed sufficient by the department's welfare officer.

We rescued a pony on Saturday, Rosie, as named by her foster family. She was living at the side of a house tied to a trailer. Rosie, like all the others, imprint on you, and you can't get them out of your mind until you can get them out of their miserable situation. The ones you don't get, they never get filed away as finished business so every now and then, their faces flash before you and the question 'where are they now?' hits you. The difficult answers your brain volunteers get quickly blocked.

Back to Rosie's rescue night! It was really dark, so it was hard to see what was what! I panicked when I saw her owner's empty hands and no Rosie. I had gone to put hay for the remaining horses in the trailer. Rosie had run up into the box by herself after getting out of her owner's hands. Let me tell you, it is what movies are made of: to see a pony that spent her days tethered being let go into a paddock. In Rosie's case, she was nose kissed by Rua, another rescue, and then she took off and ran and ran. Another shade of rescue: rewarding.

Valentine's Day will be soon here and no matter how hard I try to push 'Hay not Roses', it seems to just resonate with a few! But a lovely couple have given 100 euros worth of hay rather than gifting each other. And a friend called Jackie, stood up at the end of a Sunday sermon and talked about 'Hay not Roses' and left a bale richer for hungry horses in her area! That made me happy!

I often think what life would be like if we loved the way animals love us: unconditional and never ending. What would life be like if we bounced back the way they often do when let down by humans; what would it be like if we forgave the way they do? So we don't lose out on fully living and loving again! They are often let down so terribly by the people in their lives, yet, they still run to gates with hope, they jump up and down to be petted, and they purr with happiness.

Yes, there are at least 50 shades or more to rescuing. We just try constantly to find the silver linings around the grey. No, it's not easy sometimes.

How did it come to this? I guess LOVE. The strongest shade of rescue.

The promises we make to break

February, 2018

Promises throw me into all sorts of 'maze-like' situations and dilemmas, where I feel both ill-equipped to fulfil them and often afraid! But, in an effort to keep them, I often become both purposefully blind to danger and, yes, the humans in my life. Once I release those words, they take on a life of their own within me; they drive me on till the promise is fulfilled. Whether that is to get a horse out of a bad situation or to befriend those that are often difficult to be friendly with. I do it for them: the horses – those who are loveless, without a voice or choice where they end up.

The befriending part does not always work! I remember in Galway city feeding an emaciated cob. The owner's brother put up with me. However, he told me in very clear terms what would happen if I ever met his brother who didn't want me to feed his cob – the one he wouldn't feed himself. I still threw out those net of words to catch any chance of building a relationship the day I met him. I should have listened to his brother! It did not end well.

I try keep my promises to the horses in my life against all odds, and yet I fail miserably in keeping my promise to myself to not expect others to keep their promises to me when it comes to their horses. Yes, the problem with promises!

This week many people failed to keep promises. Some are continually breaking theirs and others have fallen at the first obstacle. An owner of three beautiful donkeys promised to feed them. He fed them for one day. An owner of beautiful mares promised he would give them water; their buckets remain empty. Then there are those whose very job is to protect the welfare of animals and to enforce the current animal welfare legislation. They don't. It seems to depend on personalities rather than their professional responsibilities whether you get help or not. Rescuers would be made redundant if the law was enforced and if those authorised to act did their job.

This week I walked down the donkeys' field late at night to get hay into their little nest they found themselves. The nest is a patch of ground surrounded by a circle of trees. I'm so afraid of the dark, that I sometimes get dizzy, if I allow all the irrational thoughts in my head to pump adrenaline through my body. But I have mastered them (sometimes!) because I promised these three furry friends I would make up for their cruel owner.

Yes, broken promises have drawn from my reservoir of tears this week. At the moment I am praying – yes, really praying that this Beast from the East breaks his promise to come here this week. So many of the horses I feed will suffer terribly with no adequate shelter.

I finally scratched the scratch-cards I was given as a Valentine's gift from a friend! Yes, call me crazy, but I never scratch cards until I feel lucky. Two out of the three cards revealed

3 stars. I wonder what would happen if I promised I would wave at you from one of the winning streak chairs? They say you should never wish for money, so I wish to write a lot of cheques for a lot of genuine, hard-working rescues and rescuers out there. Especially the ones who have come to my rescue. I would also like to pay back all the kind people who have bought hay down through the years. Now these are two promises I would like to make and keep.

This week I must get busy finding my first rescue her new forever home! My first 'rescue promise' was to her: the day I spotted her tied to a steel road-side fence, standing on muck with no feed or water. I promised she wasn't staying there. She didn't.

Telling tales or telling truths

March 19th, 2018

This week my path seemed determined to cross the paths of some people I only know because of their horses. That is all we have in common: horses they don't feed. Yes, it's ironic that horses are dying in this country because they are owned. Owners who tie them to trees in forests away from frequented pathways; owners who throw them onto bog land; owners who push them beyond their limits on sulkies; owners who give them feed that is akin to stable waste or don't provide feed, and owners who simply do not check on their horses and they die of common infections that could have been treated, or they fall into drains and experience the worst death: a slow and lonely one.

What do you do when you meet the people who steal your peace of mind? What do you say to people who own horses – horses who don't run to meet them at their gates? Arguing is pointless: to win an argument about caring with someone who has never shown any empathy is lost before it's begun. So, I talk, I half-joke, I throw in my opinion like a sprinkling of glitter with the odd sharp edge. I see their delayed reactions: did she just say that? And I smile. *Yes, I did!*

Lots of people give out to me for feeding horses. Their

misled and biased opinions believe if I feed, the owners never will. The truth is: some people won't feed their horses. That is why many fields are dotted with bones: the desperately sad evidence of starvation. Horses standing on horses that went before them in fields all over the country. What must they feel? One child said to me last week, 'did you see the new bones, Catriona?' as I threw hay over a wall! I didn't want to.

So back to telling tales. They go something like this: 'I drop them hay every day,' they say convincingly. 'That horse gets haylage and sure they never eat what I give them.' Yes, I've heard them all and I've smelt the round bales dropped into fields with diesel poured over them! Why would someone do such a thing? Because it appears there is always hay there – it's just not meant to be ate.

Last Tuesday I had to work in Galway City. I also brought hay for the motorway horses and enough to give a girl feeding two hungry ponies. I'm getting better at running from fields to a counselling room. I've learned my lesson after I was feeding one morning and lost track of time; I had an important meeting in the city. A dog running through traffic added another layer of lateness! My friend agreed to take the dog off me, and I had a change of clothes in my car but arrived at the meeting room with no shoes! Wellies didn't exactly say 'smart casual'. Yes, I did, I wore them! I laugh now thinking of my early days as a feeder, rushing to work which sometimes requires me to work in the hospital. Pre-hay bags, I would throw bales into my car, even a bale into the passenger seat, and in Galway the weather is not always agreeable to lose hay in a car. I would leave my hay mark wherever I went. It would stand out in a hospital car park!

And, back to Tuesday, the feeder in Galway wouldn't put hay in her car as she just got it cleaned! I found that so disappointing! She also wouldn't give me a landmark to find the ponies. I tried but failed to find them.

After work that day, I revisited a building that I once frequented because of work. I once worked there as a hostess and DJ. In my NUIG days, I also worked in a venue close-by for a man called Speedy who booked the best live acts. The venue changed hands many times. Those were the days when Salthill left the city behind in terms of night life. I sat in my car, filled with haylage, reminiscing until a loud knock brought me back to my present. A big smile greeted me! 'What are you doing here? And what the hell is in the back of your jeep? And what are you at now?' came cascading one after the other.

There are moments when you think, will I just tell a tale that is more digestible for him or do I tell the truth? I explained to the man I once worked with about my work and then about my 'real work'. I chose the truth.

He tripped over his words as they came out. 'What? Why would you get involved in that? And why would people not feed their horses?'

I smiled and shrugged my shoulders...because I don't have an answer – especially for his last question. I knew why I had gotten involved with horses who were in need of feed or rescuing. Before I pulled away, we both looked at the decaying building that once was (what we thought) our springboard to fame and fortune. I said to myself, how the building looked like I felt! I was permanently tired.

'I always thought you'd be something,' he said quietly as he shook his head from side to side. Wasn't sure if that was a veiled compliment. 'Well who would have predicted this one?' he looked at me with amazement.

And without thinking, I just said, 'I'm something to them, I suppose!'

I seem to be losing my 'bounce-back' feature these days but I'm still feeding. Sometimes we will fall into valleys filled with fears, doubts, and disappointments. But the key is, to climb back to the peak as quickly as possible. Find something to give you a lift back up. Even when energy doesn't allow it, you have to dig deep. I remember this great quote from one of the Cusack brothers. He said how 'it is so easy to hide away but a tragedy to never be found'. With a purpose, we have to keep going. If I gave up, many horses would be at their gates – let down by me! They are the reason I probably bounce back much quicker these days from life's other disappointments.

This morning I couldn't go feeding and my sister told me, that Nollaig, left tied in a swamp area gave out to her as she scattered hay in front of her. She was late to her. The first time I met this very weary mare, she stood on three legs: her blue rope

23

had caught in a loose shoe on her back leg when she bent down and when she lifted her head, her leg was lifted and she then somehow managed to twist the rope tight around her suspended leg. She was a mare obviously handled so very little as it was impossible for me to cut the rope. So, I drove into the site where the owners lived and kept my hand on the car horn until someone came out.

This week I'm so grateful to a lovely lady called Betty who has bought the kids in one area where I help horses some Easter eggs. When I go there to feed horses, they face the elements with me to lift, drag, and pull hay to their horses. One of these boys surrendered his pony to me. Why? Because he knew his pony deserved a life he could never give him. I'm grateful to my friends for being there the last few days and today! The snow days has literally brought rescuers down with exhaustion. I'm exhausted and I'm terribly sad but it's just 'for now'. Sad about all the horses I will never be able to rescue and sad about all the people who have let them down!

Here's to Spring and grass...I look forward to it as much as hungry horses do. I'm one step away from taking daily measurements.... but I better resist that one!

Compassion Fatigue: I'm only human after all

March,25th, 2018

I have decided two things today: turn off the weather reports when they mention 'beast' and 'east', and stop reading comments on Facebook that serve no purpose, are often not true, and definitely not kind – when kindness is really called for.

I think a lot of rescuers out there are suffering from Compassion Fatigue: very common amongst rescuers and caregivers. Rescuers are under a constant strain that comes from the often-disheartening work itself, and another layer of stress comes courtesy of critics: keyboard warriors & armchair generals! Yes, sometimes we are all guilty of taking on these roles, and often for genuine reasons like geographical distance or not having the resources to help! So, we are experts from a distance! However, there is another type of KW who is a 'fire starter': this KW likes drama and lots of it! Animals should always be the focus. If they are, we quickly would let go of petty differences of opinion or personal dislikes for each other by sharing a common goal. If we don't, the ability to rescue is minimised by our stress and frustration. self & other inflicted. We need to be mindful of how our words impact and imprint on others. Rescuers are resilient and fragile at the same time. We need to feed their resilience, not test their fragility.

Today I tried to be understanding and reminded myself that 'we're all human, we make mistakes, and say the wrong thing' to stop myself reacting and defending. But reading some comments today on one welfare page left me shocked and saddened. It was akin to being in a school playground….one without animals! Like children, adults were not minding their behaviour. Intentionally cruel at times and some comments lacked empathy – the two very things we try to eradicate and encourage in the case of the latter when it comes to rescue work.

That got me thinking of transference and projection. Something we all should be more aware of! Rescuers increasingly transfer their frustrations and anger meant for another group of people (irresponsible/cruel owners & those in authority) onto each other – and often scream from keys 'WHY ARE YOU NOT DOING SOMETHING?' – when the very people who should be doing something are off the hook! My friend made this point today on one post! It was a valid one! To quote one of my favourite songs 'I'm only human after all – don't put the blame on me!' Rescuers cannot absorb the blame others should be holding out their hands for. They are the 'somebody, do something' people who are there 24/7 when the department's and ISPCA's phone-lines ring out.

When it comes to rescuing animals – the work is never done. Moments of 'job well done' celebrations are short-lived in the rescue world as your rescue mind says, 'who's next?' Because we are living in a world now where humans not only neglect animals but are using them for their own negative need fulfilment, where they project all that they hate about themselves onto innocent animals; all they hate about the world is transferred onto the voiceless victims. The consequences are often sadistic and brutal. It is behaviour where empathy has no ground to grow in. These are the people that rescuers face in a constant and difficult tug-of-war.

Most days I witness many moments where animals display huge empathy and care. Last Summer, a wild goat was knocked down in Ennis town. I watched the other goats including their kids surround her until she passed. They cried and walked around her in circles. And when she was no more, they moved on. The now dead goat was in a field with a mare in foal who was soon due. I couldn't get anybody to help with the goat! Nobody would come to take her away. I asked the owners of the mare to help me bury her. Their reply was, 'we wouldn't eat for a week if we went near her'. So, I decided to bury her by myself. That idea itself was soon buried when I just couldn't dig deep enough. So, one hour later, I lifted gravel and a lot of compost down to her. And I buried her over the ground. It was a poignant moment as the herd watched my efforts from a distance, and the mare in foal, stayed by my side. At times she leaned her head on my shoulder. The compassion shown by the goats for their lost one, was deeply moving. The mare who stayed by my side as I cried my way through the job, along with cursing all the people who never help, was equally touching.

Yesterday I fed one of my regular little boys. It struck me how his owner doesn't even have a bucket in the field to even catch the rain that falls. If you want to know if an animal is cared for – look for buckets or troughs. They are a real tell-tale sign! This is the owner who gives the imaginary haylage every day! This little piebald on the motorway I have named Paddy is desperately lonely, but his owner who never named him wants to keep him. She never gives him feed. She just says she does!

I do think a lot of people in rescue have suffered at some stage in their life – like most. In their case, their suffering gave birth to a constant hunger to prevent others suffering! I remember a long time ago asking a fourteen-year-old girl, why she risked her life to save an animal? She replied, 'because nobody saved me!' And no, they didn't.

This week I'm grateful for Rhodiola (thanks to a thoughtful friend for pointing me in its direction!). I would highly recommend it. It gives you a constant sense of calm even when in a difficult situation.

This week I'm thinking of Joe from Charlie's Equine Rescue and I want to acknowledge his life-time commitment to rescuing horses. He thought me everything I know about rescuing horses, and I've heard the same words many times from him every time I cried or gave out whilst on the road with rescued horses, he'd smile and say, 'this is rescue!' Indeed, it is.

All is as it seems . . .

March 30th, 2018

Sometimes you just want to be wrong. In terms of rescue, you want someone to say, 'Catriona you've got it wrong! The horses you feed – well they have owners who do care; department officials do their best to enforce the law, and that welfare inspector didn't tell that consistently cruel owner that he's happy with his animals.' I'm not good at being wrong but in this case I crave to be just that: WRONG.

You see, I'm not! And you know how we can prove the first two points? I could stop feeding the horses I feed and week by week record their body score as it fades in front of me and record the lack of response from the department as they waste away. But I, like many other feeders and rescuers, can't let it get to that point of no return. How do you withdraw food and water from a starving animal? If you know, tell me! There are many cases I've reported where I can't get feed to. What has happened here? Dead bodies and bones tell you.

This week a 'thinking outside the box' friend took a huge worry from me. Feeding in a certain field meant late night visits and a ferocious fear of being caught by a farmer who just didn't want hungry donkeys to be fed. He didn't even own them! These donkeys were visited by a welfare inspector attached to The

Donkey Sanctuary. Many visits later he told me he could do no more. Even though nothing had changed for these animals. This same inspector told me they would die if they were facing a long winter and if I wasn't feeding them. The same person told me, now that it was Spring, they had a fighting chance. This is the same person who told the owner he had no concerns. One person: two very different sides. Fooling the feeder and clapping the back of the person starving his own animals. An owner who let a cow bleed to death without providing the poor animal with veterinary care (which was her legal entitlement). She died bleeding for three days. Death saved her. This case was reported to the department. Nothing happened the owner. I had to take one of his ponies from an area where possible death faced her, if left there. He sold an emaciated pony to a family who had no field or means to feed her. He didn't care. He cares about money. The appetite for it is insatiable.

If feeders and rescuers in every town and city withdrew their helping hands – we would show up an apathetic and grossly irresponsible Department of Agriculture along with all the other bodies responsible for animal welfare. Their negligence would be magnified rather than covered up by us. We are the lens to look through if you want to see the state of animal welfare in Ireland. Having a few proactive department vets/inspectors dotted around the country is not good enough for the amount of horses starving to death or suffering terrible abuse in every county in the country.

Back to this week's rescue. Yes, my friend stepped in and

did his best for these donkeys. My forever imprinted memory was when he pulled up with them at the side of the road and I opened the door. One of them shuffled over to the door and I said, 'it's over now, sweetie'. Yes, it's what magical moments are made of. He (Jack) pressed his face against mine and stayed like that until his fosterer arrived. We were no longer in the dark together but in the bright beautiful daylight where I didn't have to look over my shoulder, and he didn't have to follow a dark silhouette carrying his hay. Why can't the people paid to care just do the same?

Tonight, I'm thinking of Storm, the latest newcomer on the feeding programme. His body etched with the invisible words: neglect. Someone threw him into a soggy patch on the side of the motorway. They didn't care that no grass will ever grow here, and they cared less that directly across from a constantly busy road are two mares who stay put by their feeder. Storm wants to get to them. I leave plastic tubs when I can in these fields as I can fill a lot of water into them. If not, I leave a few plastic containers. Yesterday when I was feeding, what remained of the tubs was the twine I used to tie them to the fence. Yes, someone denied their own horses water. No, you never get used to it.

Now to the positives! Today my amazing rescue friend, Helen, sent me a video of Brogan. I rescued Brogan as a foal from a heart-breaking existence. Today I looked at a stunningly beautiful mare who bears no resemblance to the little girl who waited at many different fences and gates – waiting for help to come. It did.

Thank you to everybody who helped this week. This week donkeys are eating grass, playing in their field and hungry horses are being fed. Maslow's hierarchy of needs outlines the stepping-stones to self-actualising – becoming who we are meant to be. At the bottom is the need for feed and shelter – without these, we or they can never move to the next stage and the stage after that – each one leading to the peak of the hierarchy: 'to self-actualise'. How many owners are denying their horses their right to grow into healthy, happy, and confident horses? Too many to comprehend. My friend gifted me with a book that I've found terribly hard to put down at times this week. Titled, *Love her Wild*, it is both comforting and immensely thought provoking.

> *'. . . even on those coldest nights*
> *She could still feel the sun in the moonlight.'*
>
> Atticus

Running to stand still

May 3rd, 2018

Losing a person or animal serves to remind us of how we are at the mercy of time, accidents, disease, and even people in some cases. Death comes in many guises: with warning and without; it is natural and often it is forced before it's time on some. A tragic and unnecessary death casts a loved one or carer into the cauldron of 'if onlys' – what if we had been there side by side with our loved one – shouting their name that we are here, that we are here to protect them, that we are here to pull on life's side in their name. But sometimes we end up being apart and you are denied even playing your part in a tug of war that is 'life or death' for them.

Death had no competition in stealing Summer's heart away on Saturday. Left on a tiny patch of grass surrounded by tall concrete walls. He did his best to run from his attackers, but he ran to stand still alone and afraid. Our minds seek out the pain and fear he must have felt, and then the guilt and terribly intoxicating regret takes over. It ungrounds you because it wants to. Part of our mind likes to make us feel bad and maybe it does that to teach us a lesson, so it does not happen again. Some people must have lost this part of their mind for they neither feel regret nor do they learn lessons whilst the rest of us are nailed to a cross of worry and regret. Where Summer lived, nobody wanted her to die. I know that. But the need to own a pony without the proper facilities; the need to own a pony without regard to its safety overrides the need of the pony. They come second. What about their needs? What about the needs of all the animals tied up? What about all the breeding bitches locked away in birthing tombs? What about all the animals who walk onto ships who for weeks travel to destinations with no regard for animal welfare? *What about all of them?*

Death is a gift that does not come soon enough for them: to spend a life chained up, or tied up at the side of the road, or in darkness, is no life at all. Why do our superficial needs as humans take precedence over another's well-being or even their lives?

What has happened some people that their need fulfilment comes from causing pain, even death? What would it take to heal that part of them? Have we become too accepting or desensitised that sadistic and cruel behaviour is now a daily occurrence? Was it like this a century ago? Or is it because with access and sharing information, we just know now. I don't know.

In my mind I imagine all the other lives A Boy Called Summer could have had! I sometimes wake up and my mind plays tricks on me where I think for a second, he is still here. My fingertips feel his furry little back, and I see his big beautiful brown eyes looking for his feed. I can nearly smell him again.

It's both strange and ironic that I never made Summer a promise that I make many ponies I feed! No, I never promised him that one day he would walk out of there to a stable, a paddock and to a home. Maybe I should have.

I want to thank all the people who loved Summer, near and afar. So grateful to Linda and Siobhan who literally climbed walls to get to her as fast as they could, and to the vet, Gerry O'Connor who rushed on a Saturday night to end Summer's pain. So many people have made this pony's life and death matter. So many voices of clarity and care have pulled me from my terrible sadness and guilt.

I don't think his name will ever be forgotten now. He was a symbol of resilience and acceptance whilst he lived. Summer kept bouncing back to live life again. But last Saturday night this tiny tot could not bounce back anymore.

Here's to A Boy Called Summer, who has cast deep hoof-prints in many hearts. His death will not be in vain. That is a promise I will keep for him.

Finding Cairo in Limerick City

May 11th, 2018

When you're in the middle of 'rescue craziness' – you don't really get to stop to take it all in. Practicalities take over: the who, the what, where, why, and the whens. Mindfulness goes out the window.

You sort out the rescues in your own care, not knowing when you'll be back after you take the call. Yes, you feel guilty every time you leave them for long periods. My life is a constant runway – arriving and departing many times in one day, but I never leave the house without lipstick or lip gloss on. I grew up with a mother who believed lipstick was a great distraction to draw from other things you hadn't time for and she also saw it like war-paint!

In this case, the rescue call came from Joe (Charlie's Equine Rescue). When he says the words, 'I'm moving him today,' well – you know he means business. Joe is the kind of rescuer who just gets on with it; in believing all will be OK, it is (usually).

The 'him' was a llama who had gathered national interest given the on-going footage leaking onto various Facebook pages. Hard to watch and equally hard to turn away – because like a sad movie, you want to stay watching till the end for a happy outcome.

It never came. People were angry, upset, and calling for action to be taken. No authority responded to the calls for help, but a rescuer did. They always do.

And so, Joe arrived from Wexford, and Anna from LAW was to meet us in the city. Looking back now, as we drove there, neither I nor the driver (Pascal) pulling the box talked about any possibility of this going wrong. In fact, we didn't talk about the pending pick-up at all. Sometimes when we think too much, we can talk ourselves out of things. Sometimes it's necessary and other times not as much. But with Joe driving ahead of us, turning back was not an option. He would say, 'what's wrong with ya? It will be grand!' – if we spoke of any reservations. Before this rescue day, he had been plotting for 10 days to get this poor boy out. He just never told us till the last minute.

There is something about the urban landscape that accentuates cruelty and neglect. I constantly remind myself about how it is the luck of the draw where we end up in life and with who. As we turned into the flat and grey housing estate, I was drawn to the different mares standing over their new-borns, on flat green spaces between houses. No fence or wire to keep them in or safe – yet they stay. They know no different and when we know no different life – the one we have, becomes our 'normal' as we have no mode of comparison. This is normal to them; I wish it wasn't. I wish they had another normal.

And so, we arrived, and were met by the two sweetest greys. There is no better welcome to get. And then the owners, one by one appear. I tell them about when rescue greys arrive from Ireland to Italy – a red carpet is rolled out for them! They find this amusing. A pick-up practically brushes by me as he drives by. 'You got a box?' He shouts as he keeps his jeep in motion. One young girl passing by, asks 'why are ye taking him?' She doesn't seem satisfied with the many answers.

We were brought into a small yard, and a shed door was opened. It's surreal sometimes meeting an animal you've watched for weeks on a screen and suddenly there he is in front of you. How do you call a llama? For some reason, I called him as if he was a cat! I still don't know what sound you make, but there wasn't much calling to do; he walked from his shed leaving his shed mates behind and straight into his carriage awaiting him.

And we were off, after our goodbyes and half-joking, half-serious warnings to not go get another one! I don't think they have much interest in another one! But they did make a few jokes. 'Please, don't do that, Mr . . .' I asked!

I'm sure Cairo was relieved when the ramp came down in Clare. I'm sure I saw him smile. His fosterers led him and us through a bright red gate and into a beautiful green field. Cairo never looked back at us when his mouth found the grass and it first lingered between his teeth as he took it all in.

Joe knows no limits to what can be moved or rescued! The last time he surprised me was a call that we would be moving a dairy herd to a sanctuary in the UK. He made history in doing that and soon to follow are the sheep, the lambs, and the heifers, and calves.

This week I got to meet Rory in his rescue space with Forgotten Horses Ireland. Rory came from Ennis, where he was often tied with twine to a green railing. To see him with his rescue friends at their gate made my day. Rory had a serious accident before being rescued and that's how I met him. In nearly killing himself to escape, he threw himself and the others with him a lifeline! A call for help was made for him, and I was sent out by another rescue to help. What followed was an on-going feeding programme in this area. Every morning I drove here with great fear but with great hope. However, the day arrived when I knew I had to stop turning in. It just happens like other similar places: welcomes can be worn out when you are the one that forces it.

Bring him home

June 9th, 2018

This morning I went walking with three of my six rescue dogs to Lee's Road. Where I can walk is determined by the dogs I am with. Being able to walk here means I am with the more sociable ones: the ones less traumatised by the humans who once they shared their lives with. I often wonder as I look at them running and carefree – I wonder about the hands that fed them, cared for them, even hurt them. Jack, one of my rescue dogs avoided being rescued for many months. So many people were trying to catch him, but he told us all in his reaction to helping hands: leave me be. If only animals who run in fear, understood when there is nothing to fear.

A few years ago, on the eve of the June Bank Holiday, I posted on my Facebook page that if anyone managed to catch him, well, I would give him a home. The next morning, I was busily packing for a weekend away when I got a message, and it went something like this: 'you know the dog you said you wanted – well, last night on the way home from the pub, I saw him sleeping on the step of the friary and I just went for it. I picked him up and I wouldn't let go. When can you collect him?' I unpacked my bag.

It took Jack months to come out of a crate with an open

door when we were around. Another rescue, Dexter, stood guard at the open door. For he knew only too well what Jack had been through. Every day, another shoe was added to the wall he was building between him and his new home. He retrieved them whilst we slept. Everyday my heart broke. *'What have they done to you?'* became a daily thought and question. As the weeks passed, I got a lead on him, and he trembled and shook. I just left it on him to get used to it. One morning as I was getting the other dogs ready for their walk, I saw Dexter taking the lead in his mouth and attempt to pull Jack out of the crate. His wish for him to come could not come true because it was blocked by years of distrust and trauma. The protective wall he had built was not surmountable for the tiny part of Jack who maybe wanted to see – to see what it would be like to trust again. The risk was too much for him to take! What was important to me every day was this: Jack was going nowhere: he was home.

Years later, Jack now jumps with excitement when he hears the various leads coming off the hooks. Sometimes he still has panic attacks, and there are times when he still runs back to the car and crawls underneath. I wish I knew what he remembers. Just like us, animals can experience flashbacks and post-traumatic stress disorder. The only difference is, we can't tell them to breathe deeply, to focus on something else rather than the thought that is causing the panic, and to let the feeling pass – because it does.

Like certain memories, one song or melody resonates with

our emotional make-up at any given time. They even become 'my song' or 'our song'! The words resonate with us when we feel certain emotions or when we are faced with certain dilemmas. They can become mantras; they sometimes become painful reminders, and sometimes they fill us with such determination to keep going until we get what we want. For me, every time I meet a cat, a dog, or a horse in need of rescuing, I automatically say, 'I'm going to bring you home' – wherever that home shall be. The backing track for this is Les Misérables's 'Bring him home'. The lines, 'You can take, you can give, let him be, let him live. Bring him home . . . bring him home.' I guess there are some people who push harder in the gym when they hear their favourite work-out track; there are some people who get up out of bed in the morning with theirs, and then there are the rescuers that need something – anything, to just keep them going.

Back to the walk this morning in Lee's Road . . . as I was walking back to the jeep in the car park, a man stopped me and asked me to try catch his very sweet but hyper pointer. The dog was clever to know that it was time to go home so avoiding being caught meant he could stay longer. As we were talking, a lady appeared with three dogs and I asked her was one of the dog's named Chilli. She replied 'yes' and how she was walking them for a lady I had rehomed him to. I bent down and just said his name and he remembered. They never forget who brings them home.

The poor patient man waiting to bring Sally home was intrigued by rescue work as we talked more whilst waiting for

Sally to make an appearance. We talked about all the things we do in desperation for a cure, for a resolution, for a happy ending. Deciding what was the best way to catch Sally brought us to that topic! I told him about Erin, a beautiful mare who I found in a field years ago. One of her eyes was bleeding and her body was covered in cuts. The owners told me they had the vet out; I rang the same vet. He had not been out, so I called my vet. He told me she had a tiny percentage of vision left in her damaged eye and told me that whilst we could try treating it, she might never get her vision back. I don't know why, but I became so focused on Erin getting back her sight in that eye. I gave her everything the vet gave me. I washed her eye out twice a day and I applied the ointment and gave her antibiotics.

On one side, I was Erin's shadow; on her other side, I was the only hope she had. Each one of her wounds day by day were fading but her eye remained the same. My friend Linda told me about a Holy Well and she drove me there one day. I filled a bottle she gave me with water from the well, to bring back to Erin. I also left a few words on a tiny piece of paper and placed it amongst the hundreds of other petitions left by other hopeful and faithful visitors.

I just decided, if this was going to be it: the cure, I had to believe in it. As crazy as that might sound to some people; I chose to believe that this would give her back her sight. It did. Erin is a stunning fifteen hand mare today. We have a bond that I can't put into words. All I know is this: I am no longer her shadow. And I need to bring her home now and let her 'be' – who she was always meant to be.

Tell me what you did with your life

June 15th, 2018

It's that time of year: shy foals shadowing their mums; furry doe-eyes puppies and kittens flooding our Facebook feeds… It's all cuteness overload, well, until the 'rescue mind-set' kicks in: there aren't enough homes for all these foals, puppies, and kittens. You find yourself asking out loud to yourself, 'WHAT IS WRONG WITH PEOPLE?' A lot of these foals are a result of indiscriminate breeding; some come from older mares exhausted after making it through another hard Winter. A lot will be put back into foal soon after giving birth. Some of the luckier ones we see via rescue pages made it out of the pounds or barren fields into rescue space before they gave birth. Their filly or colt will never know the life of their parents. But what about all the others? People are breeding and they are not landowners; some invade other people's property to feed their horses. They don't provide feed in the winter, and most don't even own a bucket for water.

Animal rescuers struggle to rehome the mass number of dogs coming into them whilst councils are dishing out puppy breeding licences as if these breeders were making inanimate objects! Elsewhere, Kittens and puppies are being born into homes where their owners wouldn't know a vet clinic from the inside! It is both heart-breaking and infuriating to find kittens a few days or weeks old fighting for their lives. Their mums or dads never neutered to avoid so much suffering. And so, with human greed and selfishness, the vicious cycle of animal neglect continues – an automatic cruel inheritance – not genetic but man-made. No animal type escapes abuse and every socio-economic group is responsible for the cruelty that exists in the world.

Life is akin to a lengthy corridor with a generic start and finish line. Along this corridor are many doors. Each one is a door of choice. We have so many choices on this path to the end. As humans we are gifted with freewill. Most of us are blessed to have our full mental capacity to make rational choices. We know the difference between right and wrong! Yet, there are still those who mindfully choose 'wrong'. At the end of the day, we all get to the same finish line. But what about the footprint we leave behind? I guess, it might depend on the doors of choice we choose.

So, what is it that we need to do to make those doors of choice, that lead to cruelty, less attractive for people to enter? Hefty fines, prison sentences… what about early intervention? After all we can't really change our IQ, but our EQ can be intervened with and improved. We need to teach children to be compassionate and empathetic – to be emotionally intelligent from a young age. Those two characteristics are more an indicator of happiness and success than all the other school subjects we put so much importance on. A single time-tabled class of Social, Personal, Health education is not enough.

In the last two weeks, two rescues reinforced for me how human choices and behaviour can cause such misery, fear, and confusion in animals. A young dog was rescued from a place where the human hand was associated with pain. In his rescue space at Baby dog Rescue, the power of loving kindness caused his fear and aggression to come undone! While being petted, his big brown eyes look at his carer as if to say 'what is this? I love it!' Yes, the power of touch! Rumi was not wrong.

I was part of a rescue this week, which An Cat Dubh organised. There was a young donkey dumped in a forest and he was there for two years! It was a special rescue as when we pulled up with transport, there were many caring people waiting, to bring a donkey named Delaney home! And yes, he was going home, to An Cat Dubh!

Back to life's finish line! Beside us will be those who caused unnecessary suffering, who used and abused animals for money, who inflicted pain to distract from their own, and who got thrills out of torture for their own negative need fulfilment. What do you think that day will be like for them?

I recall a hospice nurse telling me about a man dying. No medication could control the excruciating pain that was pulling his body apart. But that concerned him less than another pain: the one caused by deep regret! It was crucifying his mind.

'I'm sorry,' he repeated and again. 'I'm so sorry,' he screamed out to the room empty of friends or family. All he had was her to listen to his cries of regret.

She asked him who it was he wished he could say sorry to. And as he took his last few breaths, he told her about a collie who stayed by his side, who remained loyal, who watched over his house from morning till night. A collie who he inflicted so much pain on. That collie took on the weight of that man's world.

Yes, we are a sum of our choices. When people choose to abuse animals, make them suffer in any way, well, that choice should be punished according to the animal welfare legislation in place. And as individuals we should never give up on an animal suffering until a resolution is reached. However, it is unfortunate that in Ireland many people log welfare concerns with relevant authorities and yet so many animals are left in situations where they are abused. It leads to complete frustration when cruelty is reported again and again, and nothing changes for the animal in need of help.

Many Cat Chapters Later

This week new neighbours moved in. Two sisters with no animals . . . just busy busy busy with take away skinny lattes doing normal life things – all sparkly about their new beginning.

Ten years ago, my sister and myself were them. We bought our house off the plans, thinking, we will sell quickly and move on again after making a profit! It was a three-storey tiny town house. The third bedroom, I once described as a room, 'you wouldn't swing a cat in it' (God only knows where that expression came from) – now is filled with climbing furniture, soft cat beds and is the bedroom for thirteen of our nineteen foster/forever cats. The small back garden is non-existent after I bid on a twelve-foot by ten-foot catio for the rescued/foster cats. I only bid on it to get the auction going at a time when I was only fostering two cats for a rescue. I guess a few years later, I am lucky I won that bid. We have six dogs who don't see eye to eye with the cats so it's dog and cat time-share with the house. The catio means the dogs get lots of walks because I feel so guilty for taking their garden away. So, it's a win-win (for them!).

Hay feeding has stopped for now but in its place is the busy job of trapping feral cats and catching kittens. Filling water

49

buckets for horses is less stressful compared to lifting square bales into your car and pulling them out at the various fields every morning and evening! Yes, one replaces the other. My back is finally recovering from the long hard winter! This week has been a busy one, mainly for my sister who is an expert trapper at this stage. One of the success stories was a 4-week-old kitten called Gobnait who decided she was staying put in a garden that was owned by a lady with a boxer who didn't take too well to a tiny ball of fur bouncing around. So, he tried his best to get rid of her and she – well, she put up a fight. It resulted in a torn mouth and a broken leg. The boxer came away with a few scratches. She was eventually caught when she got hungry enough to enter the trap. Yesterday she had surgery at Ennis Veterinary Clinic who sponsored her little broken leg being put back together with pins. She is a little confused but doing well and we did think she would lose her leg, so it was a great joy taking her home with four legs. After her recovery she will be going to live happily ever after with Katie and Cait in Clare.

But, back to the house. No, there were never any plans to have animals but one day, years ago, we decided to 'give something back' as we both were doing very well career wise and life was being good to us. I was busy working as a Guidance Counsellor in a secondary school, doing the odd show on local radio, doing freelance journalism, and doing the odd glamorous job for an agency in Dublin.

It is funny how one choice can take you down the start of

an irreversible life-path. A friend of my sister's was volunteering in an animal charity shop in town, so he told us to drop in and give him a hand. With a background in fashion and window design, I decided to do their windows every Tuesday. What I never anticipated was how I would react emotionally to the different people coming in with stories of animals being neglected and animal owners wanting to surrender their animals. And so, that is how our cat family started. A lady decided she didn't want her two cats anymore and she left them on the shop floor in a box and walked out without even a goodbye. We couldn't leave them there and neither of us had any idea how to mind a cat. We learned!

Boyfriends tend to start off so impressed by the rescue work and the horse feeding programme. I will never forget one boyfriend who totally surprised me when I said to him one very cold frosty morning, that I had to go buy hay, and he clicked his jeep open and as if it was diamonds, there before my eyes were lots of golden yellow bales of hay. No, that didn't last! You know how some people are on best behaviour in the beginning, but I will always remember the effort he went to; it was truly a lovely gift! With the other potential boyfriends, sharing my time with lots of animals became problematic and that pretty much sums up 'what went wrong'.

I have a friend who keeps reminding me that I should know how to maintain boundaries given my profession! The animal world, she constantly protests, should not take over all my life! I was never good at keeping boundaries in my own life! She made me laugh one day when she said, 'Catriona, make one room pretty and nice in your house just for you where the animals aren't allowed in!' The truth is, there is no free room! And yes, whilst I love pretty, pretty takes time!

These days, and with great honesty but maybe with a smidgen of shame, I tend to base someone's attractiveness on: being an animal lover, able to climb a tree to rescue a kitten, or having the 'know how' to load a horse, even pull one from a river! So, a few days ago, I was asked out on a date. Yes, I thought, the universe was listening to me!!! My only problem was finding something to wear, that would make it past the animals, down the stairs, to the front door, without gathering animal hair like velcro, or the material's threads being pulled by the love of my dogs and their paws. Navigating by some of my cats is like dodging cuddles with nails. They jump on your back as you pass.

So, dress to the ready, all animal stuff taken care of (ahead of schedule), I was going on a proper date! BUT . . . just when I was ready to step back into 'normal' . . . I just happened to get a little taste of my own medicine. Yes, I have often been called away to animals in need when out or often put my own animals first (ALL the time, if I'm honest!) and yes, I have really let down some lovely people along my way. I often think I will end up very lonely and without human love in my life because of my choices.

Second Chances Stolen

June 30th, 2018

They say sometimes you have to go through the worst to get to the best! These words are very apt when it comes to rescued animals: they often go through the worst days, weeks, and years to get to the best – the best life! Rescuers often make the impossible possible for some of these animals when it comes to getting them out of their dire situations. It's not always a straight-forward surrender.

We're lucky (well most of the time) because we can constantly bestow on ourselves and others the magical 'second chance'. We can forgive, we can move on, we can change, we can leave, we can begin again…. we are in control usually (if only we all realised that). It is like switching a channel because we don't like what we are watching, we can switch the scenes of our own lives with time and with effort. Then again sometimes it's only 'parts' of our lives that need 'up-lifting' or 'redecorating'. Parts are easier to change than everything. Sometimes we get overwhelmed when we think everything is wrong. Our thinking is not always right!

The heatwave has brought with it a new wave of pressure on rescuers and volunteers! Yes, it goes from 'nothing to eat' for some horses to 'nothing to eat or drink'. I think one of the saddest things I've seen this week is a pony licking the drops from a plastic bottle that some passer-by cruelly threw over the gate! As she moved and squashed it a few drops came out. I was so happy to produce a bucket and water for her. She was grateful; they always are. I tend to keep my head down and get on with it when I have to pull up alongside busy roads and lift water and buckets out. So, to do it, I just block out the cars slowing down to see what you're doing because I find it hard. I don't really know why, but on one of these days this week, I got really angry; I pulled up on the hard-shoulder and watched a small pony wobbling from side to side, and I watched her fall. Getting over council wire fencing is never easy as it's so hard to squeeze your foot into those tiny, diamond green spaces, and in PE in school I was never good at scaling the jumps. So, not only did I have to do it once, I had to do it three times as with panic I didn't bring all I needed at once. On the other side of the fence, cars continued to slow down to see was the pony OK. Nobody asked – apart from two curious Guards in a passing patrol car.

I don't know what it is about passers-by – well some anyway, when you're with horses that are not yours! It brings out the best and the worst in people; you remember both. Like the very assertive cyclist this Winter who cycled up to my car and bellowed, 'it's about time you fed her' as I lifted a bale of hay out of the passenger seat. The words wouldn't come out quick enough, 'but she's not mine!'

Back to second chances. . . many were dished out this week and two were taken away. Like Gobnait, the now 7-week-old kitten who is now walking away with two pins holding her leg together. And a little dog who has had more litters than the owners can remember was spayed and returned home. A second chance of life without always being a mommy! Fionn, a stunning stallion, came up in my memories today. He once lived a very lonely life in Ennis. When he was a foal, I found him sleeping in a circle of rushes, that he had made his home. He was so very afraid of everything. To see him now: a regal and proud gelding in Germany, well, it reminds me, it's worth fighting for those second chances. Life I guess will always offer us a second chance if we are lucky enough; it's called tomorrow.

What to do with a broken heart?

July 6th, 2018

If I was an independent production company and wanted to produce cheap television with maximum impact, I would stick a few mics and cameras on rescuers! 'Keeping up with the rescuers' – let me tell you it would be hard to! In 24 hours so much can happen that when you lay your head on the pillow – you feel you've lived a week!

Yes, this week I watched fellow rescuers practically jump from one county to another – going with one and coming back with more animals! I did home-checks, rehomed, and I experienced a sad failed home. This week has been an emotional rollercoaster with the setting on 'high speed'. On one of the days, I took a rescue kitten for her first vaccination as she was going to her new home later that day! Quickly got her in and out, home to take care of the 29 animals in my own house, 2 sets of walks with 6 dogs to two different areas, litter trays cleaning, cat feeding, and meds, and then it's water filling and dropping, back to do a very quick change for work. Finding work clothes amidst the wardrobe chaos is so stressful. I'm making it a priority to have outfits ready to go! If I was judged on my professional attire, I'd never get any work!

One of my session's was coming to an end, when I looked at my client and said 'oh, no, Prince Harry!' I won't begin to tell you his reaction. I tried to gather my things politely but rapidly as Prince Harry had a 4:15 appointment at the vets which was very important! I nearly forgot it! PH being an older kitten who had to have most of his teeth removed. So, getting into the catio with a box sends all the cats into hiding but the Prince was quickly spotted hiding 'not very well' in the grass! Poor PH – the vet says his mouth is so very sore still! And then home to the same cycle, of walks in shaded areas and more water filling! And then. . . the letting go!

This is a part I'm not good with. Putting the rescue kitten into a cat box, we made our way to meet her new human mommy! I stood in the hotel foyer and took her out of the cat box as it was too hot outside to wait. And I held her, and told her how brave she was, how loved she was, and how lucky she was to have been rescued. She dug her little claws into my neck and snuggled in as she was so unsure of all the new hotel sounds. After a few minutes, her new owner arrived with open arms and I let go of another heart-beat – her paw print etched into my heart forever!

I wish my past-self knew all those times my heart was broken that to get busy living is the best distraction and remedy for that raw and debilitating emotion of loss: the letting go and saying goodbye! Yes, I cried but when I got back into the jeep, there were three messages about animals needing help: the type of messages that are the Kleenex for rescuers! They quickly dry your eyes and push you on! Loss is inevitable but it's how we react to it that determines how we will be. Yes, we have to feel the emotion, but we can't stay in the damaging darkness alone with our thoughts. We're better off staying connected and busy.

Yesterday, I had to cancel sessions in Galway as what is usually a run of the mill visit to Erin, turned into a few hours in a dried-up dusty field, trying to stay calm as she got more stressed! Every time I left her to get something from the jeep, I could nearly hear her say, 'don't leave me, I'm afraid!' So, I got a head collar on her and a lead rope from the jeep and we walked and talked. And, as you suck up your emotion, so she won't sense it, part of you gets ready to let go. Part of you sends this quiet message to your brain… she might die here! It's the 'here' that cuts the deepest! I can't bare the thoughts of any of the horses I've spent years feeding and caring for dying in these 'killing fields' of nothingness! No water in the Summer and no feed in the Winter! I called my vet but there was no answer, so I resorted to prayer – yes, prayer! Like the day I found her bleeding and partially blind, I prayed for her! So, after a few hours, she kind of told me, she had enough of me, and whatever was hurting her, stopped, and she walked away from me and looked back once as if to say 'I need to be alone now!'

So, I let her be and went home but drove by twice before I left for Galway City. I don't know why Erin has not had the same luck as other horses I've gotten out! I'm trying but for some reason, the universe is keeping her here.

There is going to be another emotional goodbye in a few days – although my rescue friend, Katryna, always tells me, never say, 'goodbye'. My friend Lorraine has been taking care of four very special rescues, Peaches, Ludeen, Leo, and Daisy. Peaches & Ludeen were rescued by SCAR from an incredibly terrible life of constant abuse. I ended up having to rescue them from the home they were put in. Where a man believed you could beat the stallion out of one of them! Peaches was gelded all the time! And then two further homes did not work out until I found Lorraine. Then along came Leo. There are not enough words to describe this bundle of sweetness. When I met him where he was kept, my heart nearly broke. There he was – with nothing but a big swollen belly. The vet was called and there was a chance he had ragwort poisoning. So, after weeks of feeding, on those grounds, the owner surrendered him, along with his friend, Daisy, who was meant to survive on the moss growing from the concrete!

So, it happened very quickly in the last few days, that three ladies in Wales offered them a forever home together. Lorraine has been working so hard getting various things ready for them to leave. Whilst Joe has arranged the transport with Castlepark. These four 'not goodbyes' will be very testing but more so for Lorraine and her family.

I'm not sure what there is left to say about the water situation! Some people say to me, 'shur, they won't give water if you give it!' I've stopped defensive reacting to such comments!

But all I know is – that during the week, with the heat and lifting, I reached exhaustion! I took out my phone and took a picture of myself to capture this moment! It frightened me but it has passed now! I desperately want to get back to my own life, so if there was a slight chance that owners I know would take responsibility – I would be simply relieved. But, they won't! In fact, with some owners, I have to sneak in water, and they have no idea where I have buckets hidden. There are no buckets or containers left by them in these fields to catch the water that just might fall again soon.

I often wonder what would happen if all the rescuers in the country gathered in one big venue. What would the most prominent emotion be? I know when I meet some, we spend the first few minutes doing the familiar 'giving out', sharing the difficult stories, and what is left after that is the 'happy stuff': the shared stories of new homes and successful rescues.

Rescuers are doing a really difficult job out there. They are doing it – not for nothing: they are doing it for sentient beings with no voice or no means to help themselves. They exist in the absence of a proactive reaction and intervention by authorities when it comes to animal welfare. They exist 24/7; they don't stop at the weekends or after five on weekdays. I'm just 'small fry' when it comes to rescuers, and I'm in awe of the ones out there that defy all sorts of impossibilities that come their way. They truly make the impossible possible for some animals!

Changing minds, changing lives

July 15th, 2018

It takes more than a key to unlock some doors: you have to unlock minds first. The last few days were given over to a rescue that was both challenging and complex. The animal/s never pose any problems; the humans who own them do. It often takes so many people to undo man's cruelty to just one animal. It's like a tug of war: there may be more people on the rescue side but the stubbornness and cruelty of one owner is a fierce force in itself. It's never an easy win and losing is something you have to suck up pretty quickly sometimes.

Negotiating is sometimes as exhausting as the fight, and maybe I should learn to just skip the part I often try: 'let's talk about it'. Talking is futile when some people's minds are locked and set in their ways. So, during the week, two rescues and myself stood together (probably in shock) as we faced a person whose next words would decide the fate of the animal you have by your side, waiting to leave. And sometimes you run out of 'cards to play'; your mind searches for something, anything that will ensure the animal's freedom. Yes, sometimes what you say can be a gamble: it might win over one person and make an enemy of

61

another. It depends on the mind doing the processing.

Yes, the rescue was successful, but one rescue like this can often lead to people saying, 'wait till I tell you….' It's those telling tales that haunt you and tinge the successful rescue: the animals that came before this one. I think we all felt like we had been hit by a machine gun of words – such was the effect on us all and in particular one. We are all exhausted, and my poor nephew yesterday tried to hold open my eyes with his little fingers to watch his favourite programme with him! That's what was important to him!

And to the good news, four little rescues from Clare made their journey to Wales safely where they will live out their lives together with three lovely ladies but prior to that, they will spend time with the knowledgeable and kind-hearted Helen to get them ready for their new home. One remains so nervous even after two years of being rescued! Time does not erase some 'human inflicted' mental scars.

It was wonderful to see Rory again, one of the ponies that was on the Winter-Feeding Programme last year, looking so well with Forgotten Horses Ireland. I think the before and after picture says it all. Sometimes when you're feeding these horses, you build these very fake relationships with some owners, hoping that some of them might just release the horse to you. In Rory's case, it was an eleven-year-old boy who let him go. I can't put into words what tethered horses go through every day. There is something about that rope that kills their spirit and their hope. It's that rope that 'ties' them to you. You can't get them out of your mind. As the days went on, Rory's head barely lifted when I arrived with feed. Yes, it is one of the most difficult emotions to deal with: loving a person or an animal that can never be yours. I tend to say it a lot! The heart finds it hard to accept the aching message the mind reluctantly sends it: 'let go'. Rory is one of the lucky ones. I have failed many, many others. I'm so grateful to Forgotten Horses Ireland for giving Rory this wonderful life whilst he awaits a new forever home.

The last few days of Facebook's newsfeed doesn't give you much hope for mankind's mindset when it comes to animals! A foal, maybe two days old navigating his way through urban life in Dublin. A woman walking her dog in the park but walking back to her car with the dog by the throat. And so many dogs stolen from loving homes and families. Horses and foals without water and kittens running onto motorways in search of their mommies who left them to keep them alive to get food. It's sometimes too much for us to see: imagine what it's like for them?

And the good news ... a very spirited and determined woman I know has set a goal: to open a horse sanctuary. She already has one of her own, but this would be akin to the scale of the donkey sanctuary! If you visited her own rescue/sanctuary, you would feel a real sense of healing, help, and hope. Perfect paddocks with horses who share one thing in common: they were all rescued from some of the most terrible of places. But here, they all get that golden ticket 'to begin again' and it's as if this woman unties their pain body and leaves it outside the gates to this haven for animals. Yes, her dream may be BIG, but the horses who are being let down by their owners and authorities need something like this because rescues are full to capacity and some horses can never be what they once were: sometimes the wounds and emotional scars that their owners inflicted on them means the only solace is sanctuary.

My 'letting go' of my former life meant surrendering three large bags of clothes to Marda's charity shop in Galway City yesterday! Letting go of the clothes is easier than letting go of the memories that might never be again. But as a lady said to me during the week, 'of course you will never have those times back, but there is nothing stopping you creating new ones!' I just won't be doing it in sequence or sparkle!! Which reminded me of a quote I read when visiting a person in recovery, 'we can't go back and create new beginnings, but we can start today to create different endings!'

No, we can't erase the terrible beginnings some animals endure, but in rescuing, we change their endings. That is a guarantee.

More than a picture

July 21st, 2018

'I walk down memory lane because I love running into you.'

Yes, not only do pictures speak a thousand words but they also trigger many memories and an array of emotions. Sometimes when we cry, we are not only crying for what the photo has captured, we are crying about its context – what the camera didn't capture. Yes, we have to mind all our emotions that often get triggered by one picture!

There are so many good animal stories to write about this week. Yesterday my friend helped me transport a rescue pig to My Lovely Horse Rescue. Once she walked down the ramp into her enclosure, and when she realised where she was, she turned in circles, skipped, and smiled as she went from one corner to the other taking her new freedom in. And then there was a special welcome from another pig. I have looked at the pictures on my phone repeatedly! So happy, relieved, and sad – all at once! The latter emotion is respectfully for those that will never know something we take for granted: fresh air. I think most people have a 'the one that got away' memory. Rescuers have hundreds of them.

Two hours previous to this the predominant emotion was frustration when this cutie put up a right fight not to get into her transport. But, once in Kildare, the sun shone on her and her love for life as she ran around was infectious – why would we as people deny this to so many others? I guess it's when 'I want' comes before 'them'. It was great to see another two pigs I rescued from a petting farm being loved and adored here. Rescuing this pig from a completely dark shed with no bedding was not easy. It took four of us and a difficult hour of persuading a very stubborn owner to let her go. This little pig – now called Tina Sunshine, was being hidden from the world outside and the world outside had been stolen from her.

And then there was Caoimhe this week who was trapped. A young cat worn out from having litters. I don't think I ever saw a cat so very sad. But one photo pales into insignificance when her new home sent me a photo of this little rescue looking nothing like the cat we first trapped. She was content and happy. Caoimhe certainly knew home life before she found herself living the difficult life of a feral cat.

I've noticed the last few mornings I wake up and silently I ask 'what is there to worry about today?' so starting tomorrow morning, I'm going to try ask 'what do I not have to worry about today?' The last few days I have been worried about many animals including Erin who had to have her hooves done. I was worried how she would cope with a man that close to her and would I have a death of a farrier on my conscience! Earlier I watched her walk away with her head down when she saw Gerhard (The Friendly Farrier) at the gate with me. I wanted to say, 'we'll leave it' rather than traumatise her. Before this moment, I had to go up to another section of this area and call her to the gate. And when she came running, she was breathtakingly beautiful. Her two big brown healthy eyes smiling with anticipation. Little evidence of her previous blindness.

So, one hoove at a time, she stood quietly listening to myself and Lorraine talk, and she ate from a bucket. We had some sedative on standby and if it was fit for human consumption, I would have had it – such were my nerves! The last time Erin had anyone near her hooves, was to shoe her for a sulky. Her memories of that time are very much like a photo album flicking constantly in her mind. Sometimes I can see her go back there. She gets angry at me if I clink something too loud and she'll just hang her head and walk away, or if a box passes on the road, she hides. There is no intervening in this reaction – but it passes … the fear relived all passes if we let it without panic or resistance. I wish she knew that.

Three puppies came to my attention this week. And it is truly amazing what happens when you look for help on Facebook. It's like casting out a web of need and watching many people connect and respond with offers of lifts or rescue space. These puppies: their mommy survived constant abuse and her luck changed, the day her family left their rented accommodation and left her behind. For months she slept under a mobile home and nobody could touch her or coax her out, but one man did, and he slowly gained some of her trust. She is still wary but sleeps in his shed now so that's a start! So, thanks to HART rescue, her babies will only know care and love.

And then there is Jill Smith, the 'giving back' farmer from Cork. I heard on a Newstalk show this morning that the average young person will take 25,000 selfies in a lifetime. And the show went on to talk about 'getting work done' and improving people's lives in doing so. All of this 'fixing' really got me thinking of Jill. I took her picture prior to her cows being loaded for Hillside Animal Sanctuary. I captured a woman who radiates purity of kindness and compassion. She spoke into the TV3 camera with no words of 'how's my hair?' or 'can I see how I looked?' Her very sense of self and being is born from and energised by her love for life and her animals. The heavy burden of superficiality has no home in her. She symbolises 'being'. Just be as you are because that is enough. She is enough and more, just as she is. The only work Jill has ever got done is the hard work of running a farm by herself. How lucky these animals are compared to those who left for Libya this week from Cork. After they were loaded, and a prayer was said for Jill and her animals, we drank tea around an open car boot. It was the nicest tea I ever drank.

A fellow rescuer and a friend asked me yesterday as we sat around a table, how come I don't give my rescue work a title/a name? The answer is both simple and complex. I guess when we give a name to an animal in need, you quickly attach to them. In the same way when we like someone and we find out their name, it swings back and forth in your mind, which makes sense of the saying 'I can't get them out of my mind', so for me to give my rescue work a name would make it official and I always have a sense that I'm just passing through this rescue world and any day now things will be better for animals, and we will all be made redundant. Being an empath and a rescuer is like being a pin cushion: the pins are endless. It's hard to endure.

When I had my fortune told years ago, I had no pets in my life. Yet, the reader of my fortune could only see me with horses. There was nobody and nothing else. To-date everything she predicted which was completely irrelevant at the time has come through except for one event. Maybe no matter how hard we try, our life's purpose, like hide and seek, ready or not it will find us.

Living on a prayer

Sometimes as a rescuer, as in life, the serenity prayer are the only lines to 'go to' to equip you for life's dilemmas. Here you get reaction reminders – when to have courage, acceptance, or wisdom. Without knowing it, I'm beginning to live it because I have to. So how did they play out this week?

On Monday my first rescue, Mini Ellie, went to her new home. This home knew it would be unfair to have her by herself, so they picked the perfect friend for her: Robin, a Forgotten Horses Ireland rescue. And so, we were picked up by them and we made our way to Croom. It's never easy to let go, but I surprised myself when I never cried. Something in me knew, she was finally home, and both of us had reached our final parting point. And accepting that was part of my letting go with ease. I guess to keep any rescue forever is often like watching your front garden grow so beautifully but the back garden is crying out for attention! There are other rescues needing you. So, you turn your back on your hard work and let someone else enjoy it. Mini Ellie's new family truly love her already. I guess we have to be able to let go of people we love too sometimes. Acceptance is a remedy for the arrow of pain through your heart. Accepting that it is for the best and accepting that the pain will ease with time. It works!

Then it was music to my ears when Joe from FHI said on the way home, 'we will move Erin', to join my friend's old mare who was heartbroken to see her field buddy go. Blue mothered Mini when I first rescued her. At 36 she made a great mother to a pony who had seen too much hardship for a two-year-old.

But Erin's move was not meant to be. Erin is now a tall beautiful mare but a mare afraid of her own shadow. I was so proud of her as she bravely went in step by step; I held the lead rope ahead of her. I looked at the bar thinking once I get behind that, she will be in fully and the ramp can come up. And so, I ducked under as her last reluctant hoove made it in enough that the ramp could be lifted back up. But it was at that point, her fear memory must have been triggered and she panicked. Erin was determined to get back out. I can't tell you how it happened, but I didn't get a chance to tie her to keep her facing forward. All I remember was seeing her legs kicking every side of the box, and my fingers letting go of the lead rope.

Once back out, we all tried to pacify her to keep her calm. And then, you hear the words that make you want to cover your ears. 'NO, please No,' nearly escaped me. But you surrender to the wisdom of another rescuer who knows best. And so, you accept the words, 'we'll have to let her out!' And the ramp comes down and you watch her running away from you only to come back with eyes full of regret. If she could talk, she would have said, 'bring back the box and I will try again. Let me try again!' We all know that feeling, knowing we need to face our fears in order to move forward. But we will try again. One day, Erin! One day! Your day will come!

I guess some rescue ponies are like boomerangs: they keep coming back. Peaches, Ludeen, Leo, and Daisy were brought back from Wales. At least they got to use their passports this year! I have learnt homes can pass strict home checks and still surprise you with their unsuitability.

This week Facebook was filled again with terrible accounts of animal cruelty. I really try to understand, even feel compassion for the person so broken and hurt that they can inflict such pain on another living being. But anger overcomes you most of the time – however, wishing them pain does not bring the animal back to life. Do we pray for these people or do we curse them? Which helps the most?

Every week I make a real attempt to try fit in 'exercise'. I need to face this Winter stronger and fitter. Last Winter I could feel my back giving in as I lifted bale after bale. So, after some research I decided CrossFit is exactly what I need. Getting there is the only obstacle I face now. I'm looking forward to it though.

This week I realised how lucky I am to have great men in my life that will help me. I probably take the great women for granted as they are constant and forever. Whether to transport, to build shelters, or to listen to me – yes, I have great men in my life!

When human nature becomes undone

August 13th, 2018

What can you say that hasn't been said already after watching the horrifying clip of a young man throwing and kicking a tiny kitten around – this was after putting her on a hob. Maybe we should be asking questions like: why are young men kicking a kitten around instead of a football; why are they posting these video clips as badges of honour; what part of them is so broken that this is how they try to fix their brokenness, and what part of them finds kicking around an 8 week old kitten amusing – so much so, that you can hear a chorus of laughter behind the camera!

One of the diagnostic criteria for sadism is 'getting pleasure from inflicting pain'. Therefore, shouldn't these young men be flagged by mental health services as requiring emergency intervention and shouldn't they face a charge for intentionally inflicting harm on an animal? Will any of those things happen? If they don't – do you think people who have this in them, stop by themselves? The answer is a regrettable: NO! When people cannot control their harmful and anti-social behaviour – is it not the job of authorities and relevant public bodies to do so?

This morning I woke up adamant to get on top of things: feeding, vet visits, and getting ready for the pop-up shop. As I was

73

putting one foot into my boots, I was skimming through my newsfeed. I saw 'Clare & graphic content'. What sprung automatically to my mind was a post by Baby Dog rescue the previous night outlining how there is cruelty in every part of Clare. One man questioned that. I can vouch for it. There is. And I sat down, one foot in and one foot out, and my hand reached my mouth as I felt physically sick watching an innocent baby being abused by a young man who proceeded to whip off his shirt as a premiership footballer would do after scoring a goal! This young man wasn't scoring any goals – only the applause and approval of his friends watching on. I quickly looked for a number to call. Like many of us who saw it – your instinct is 'I have to find him!' And so, I did, with the help of MLHR who worked at a fast pace to secure a phone number that would lead to rescuing this kitten.

Getting on top of things pales into insignificance when all you can think of is a tiny body enduring the boot of a young man. Kicking him with full force; tossing him into the air with no regard for the tiny bones that would make impact with a tiled floor. You could nearly see his insatiable appetite for more and you could certainly hear it from his friends.

As I drove to the house to get the kitten, I glanced at the empty cat box in my driver's seat. Hoping he would be there and praying no minds would be changed.

I was so grateful that on my way home, there was a box with the most adorable kitten inside. Before reaching Ennis, I stopped the car, opened the door and took him out to cuddle him as he was crying. Once held, his cries stopped but there was no purring, just silence; there was no resistance, just a little body giving in, nearly waiting for what was to come.

Today, I have seen every aspect of the human character: anger, outrage, sadness, kindness, apathy and dismissal and a disregard for what really matters. You see, this kitten matters. It's not just about this tiny vulnerable pet; it's about every other kitten, dog, horse and farm animal that is abused. It's about the lack of appetite for justice from some of those in authority. Without justice we are allowing sadistic, disturbing, and self-gratifying behaviour to take the place of 'normal'. Without normal we continue to spiral into a place where laws and morals are nothing but words – weak and irrelevant words. We cannot minimise the pain of animals. To dismiss their suffering makes it OK to cause it. None of us want that, surely? Yet, so many of us are desensitised to the suffering of animals.

In the last few days, this is my experience of authorities when I went to them on different matters of cruelty: 'I must have missed that day in Templemore,' one member of the Guards told me when I reminded him he is an authorised officer to intervene in cruelty when we presented him with a clear cruelty case. Infront of his desk, I showed him a small dog in my hands with a wire wrapped around her leg to sever it as she walked. I told him where I got the dog. He did nothing. She died. With another cruelty case, I was told to just 'let it go'. Today what happened this kitten was dismissed initially as 'lads just being lads'. This type of 'lad' is not the type of 'lad' I want any animal crossing paths with. One Guard actually called me to tell me to return the kitten: to a house where abusers frequent. My answer was: NO.

Tonight, this kitten is safe; she should have been safe in her own home. Last night a group of young men chose to put her life at risk. They chose to inflict life threatening kicks and throws, and they chose to film it. It is time our justice system set precedents.

Every day is one little life

September 2nd, 2018

There are those life certainties that can trigger all sorts of complex emotions. One of these is getting older. No cream, no injections, nothing can subtract years from us really. It can be disguised, delayed – maybe distracted for a while with a sign that could read, 'move on, not welcome here!' Age tends to get around those resistances. It's a right pest and it's persistent. I never really worried about getting old(er) and even my friend's reaction yesterday, 'Oh S&&t,' when I told her what age I will be next week – well, it leaves me totally unphased. I'm fine with getting old; it's akin to getting out of bed early in the morning: I don't want to, but I have to get up and get on with it! Acceptance in key. But getting old has begun to worry me for a host of other reasons. Lifting bales and holding on to unhandled horses – well I'm managing it (for now); I'm just not sure if my back can take many more years.

Yes, rescue work has moulded me and conditioned my mind in ways I never would have foreseen. I no longer change 20 times a day to only return to the first outfit of choice. From Sunday to Thursday it's choosing whatever comes first out of the 'rescue wardrobe'. What I wear matters so little to me now: fashion is just a word and a choice. I never get time to ruminate on the 'whys' that consumed my younger self: 'why doesn't he like me? Why has he not called? Why didn't I get that job? Why is he unfaithful? What's wrong with ME?' Yes, the questions arise, they hurt but rescue work pushes the button called 'next' constantly and the word 'I' moves from the centre of my world and with that movement comes a life (ironically) less stressful and less selfish. Irrational thoughts are often generated by the 'I' word. Rescue work requires a heap load of common sense and rational solutions.

But then there are kids and the ageing issue! Yesterday, a friend and I stood in a field surrounded by kids and horses – lots of them. I can't move here without a kids' chorus of 'Catriona, can you…' I'm a softie and 'Yes, I can…' is nearly always the answer. The wish to give them what would make them happy is huge. They don't ask for much! Just the wellies off my feet!! This area started off as a 'I don't think I can go in there' place to 'we've gone in and done what we set out to'. It's a good feeling knowing that there is a mare with a foal able to walk again. Her overgrown hooves were going to kill her. We managed to separate her and her foal from the herd – still unsure how we managed it in an area of at least 15 acres. And the farrier arrived and worked his magic after Pascal managed to catch her and halter her. I could not have managed this by myself.

Back to the kids: another certainty as you grow older as a woman is the decreasing chances of ever being a mommy. But again, lately when I'm distracted by mommies and their daughters hand in hand, the phone will ring or beep and the lingering maternal feeling of 'want' is extinguished by any of the following 'they need….hay, wormers, the vet, you…'

I guess there are other ways your maternal or paternal instinct gets fulfilled. Like when you nurse a kitten in your arms – who just wants his own mommy. Yesterday morning, little Toby passed away. Found all on his own outside a vets, he was taken to SCAR. Seeing his tininess in a run made me bring him home. He went from playful and vocal to still & silent. And I knew like all the other kittens who can one day be full of life and the next day be still and silent that Toby's hours were numbered. But he was taken to the vet who made the kindest decision for him. No, you never get used to it, nor do you get use to the cruelty and sheer disregard for welfare of animals. Toby was born because somebody somewhere did not neuter their cats! Animals have so many choices removed from them. They need responsible owners to make the right choices for them. This morning Toby's crate is in the garden to be disinfected and all his favourite colourful mice are not being played with. I can't bare the thoughts of him never being cuddled again or never getting old. Getting old is denied to so many of us and animals and yet we resist it – it's a curse for some – but maybe a true blessing in disguise we need to be grateful for. Some people and animals are not blessed with growing old.

Being part of many rescue & welfare groups on FB – what

struck me yesterday was the constant beeping alerting me to new conversations. These conversations are so energised, so spirited, so eager to rescue. These women (yes, mainly women) from morning till night face down so many challenges, and they network at high speed in order to get homes for unwanted animals or safe places for animals at risk. I'm in awe of them.

These mornings I wake up thinking about a dog who so badly needs a human to help him. Last night I fed him late and in the dark I couldn't see him through the rickety gate as I pushed his food under, but I could feel his nose as he leaned on my hand – so desperate for human contact. He rapidly licks my hand to try keep me there. Such a loving dog deprived of all he needs. Rumi said there is power in touch.

This week I'm so grateful to everybody who helped me. Pat and Pascal for donating endless hours to the animals and reminding me 'all will be OK'. They put up with my fiery side which is easily ignited and is not so easy to deal with. If they ever leave me and the animals, I would have to put out an advertisement with a long list of qualities they have. I will just leave out one or two maybe!

The problem with obsession

September 13th, 2018

I live in a small house and yes, I probably have too many animals. We bought the house when we had no animals, and lack of wardrobe space was my biggest worry for the masses of material with tags I had accumulated. Today only six of the animals are mine, and the rest are long-term fosters or cats from a rescue they couldn't go back to. I often put up posts asking for foster homes, but they never come and so it's a case of 'getting on with it' and making the best of a small space with many animals. It's ironic how people say 'you can't take another one' – well, they never even take just one from me. But just because I do, doesn't mean they have to. I'm learning to manage that trigger.

So, a catio twelve feet by eight was put into the garden to give the rescued cats a sense of normality. It took away half the garden from the dogs. So, they are given two 45-minute walks a day. The day starts at 6:00 (we are trying earlier) to make sure all the rescues start the day with a clean disinfected space, their meds (if prescribed) and food and toys. Is it easy? No! Is it necessary? Yes! Would I have it any other way? Yes! But. . . Rescues are over-loaded, and I think in this house we are reducing the burden for one of the bigger rescuers. The craving for a house out the country is unbearable at times and I find myself stalking other people's country houses and imagining 'if only…' I have now decided to stop ruminating over the people whose selfish and disturbing behaviour feeds into the vicious cycle that is rescue. We exist because their moral compass doesn't. We exist because a lot of animal owners have serious psychological disturbances, so much so, they use animals to transfer and project their issues onto. We exist because of the greed out there. The greed that says to them, 'I have to have. . .' And so, they use animals to feed their insatiable selfish needs and wants. Unless you meet them in a therapy room or until the laws are consistently enforced, their behaviour continues with great ease.

This week I had a conversation with someone about 'if you bring kids into the world…' well, sometimes you must deny yourself many things as they must come first. Time is one of them. I chose or gave in maybe, to foster and rescue, and when you sign up to do those two acts, you must 'roll with it' and what it entails. Some rescues do a great job rescuing and then they do a very poor job of maintaining the welfare and well-being of the very animals they have given refuge to. Fortunately, there are just a few of them. It's not easy to take care of a lot of animals but you make it manageable. You have to manage your own life better to compensate for the time that needs to be given to them. This is another area I'm working on. Yes, you can easily get lost in the rescue world; you can quickly lose sight of your life that was, before rescuing. It becomes akin to some far-off tourist destination that suddenly you don't mind if you never visit again. Sometimes I find myself even boasting to friends of my life before rescuing – I'm not sure why! But you miss it less and less because your love and drive for animals and their welfare takes over. There is an Arabic word called 'Zahir' which means when you become so obsessed with something you forget about everything else. This state is no good for the animals and it is a state I and others must try and avoid 'full-time'! How do you do that? You move with ease between the two worlds: the rescue world and the world your family and some friends (those that survive your Zahir!) exist in. You stop resenting when they too need time or even when you have to go to work or even go out and socialise. Animals can survive without being a 'Velcro Rescuer'. If you don't mind yourself – well, they one day will suffer from your complete love and devotion for them. You will be a shadow of yourself and shadows are of no use to anyone. So, there are times when you have to come off Facebook, there are times when you have to go out, dress up, and feel human. And there has to come a day when you stop being a tourist to your own life!

It's hard to be positive amidst the terrible stories of animal cruelty. I'm thinking of the family cat shot in MoonCoin in Kilkenny. I'm thinking of Tiny who was stolen from his loving home in Tipperary. I'm thinking of all the animals held somewhere where their welfare is at risk. I'm over-thinking about the recent seizure in West Clare. What could have been is haunting.

The last few days I've watched Erin who I feed and love dearly limping badly around her field. Unable to halter her meant the vet who came could not examine her. A friend tried but she was not entertaining a human coming near her. This is Erin, a mare who up until recently would place her head on my shoulder as I stood by her gate. The last few days she has tried her best to hurt me with kicks and bites. She is angry. The trust I built up with her was snatched by her 'owners' and replaced with 'fear' – literally overnight by something they did. They hurt her again.

On a positive note, my friend visited her yesterday to find her as the previous night I couldn't and in my efforts to, I fell down a slope in her area and smashed my phone. A modern-day frustration is unable to answer your iPhone or make a call thanks to a few screen cracks. But she let him pet her. She's on her way back to trusting again and that is gold.

This week I'm also grateful to friends in my life that keep me grounded and that is no easy task. I'm grateful to you for reading this and you never know, this blog might just make the finals in Ireland's Blog Awards 2018. But we'll take the shortlist for now.

Typing this at the vets with a little kitten called Joey on my lap purring. It's really great to be here for kittens just like him. It's great to just be here.

Fairy tales are man-made

September 21st, 2018

Sometimes you have to keep trying till their last breath is stolen from them and you. . .

Lately my defiance and stubbornness to not give up becomes quickly replaced by an unfamiliar apathy and acceptance. There is no conscious choice, it just happens. It's a 'lately' thing. I'm hoping I can resume my defiant state full-time soon. Apathy is my idea of ugly.

My heart was broken yesterday when my sister rang me to say that Joey had died at the vets. Joey was a very ill kitten but after his first appointment and getting what he needed, I decided he was going to live. No, it is not a God Complex: it is simply wanting a kitten to grow old, and everything in between. But in rescue, there are no magic wands. He was the best patient and accepted all the food syringed into him. And so began a tug of war between life and death. The latter won. I loved him very much.

So many kittens are born in this country every year; so many suffer the pain and fear none of us as adults could manage. Throughout the last few days before being admitted to the vets, he never stopped purring. And in an effort to not be alone he would jump out of his bed and face the door to walk out with me every time I left his room. When you feed an ill animal or a person and as you watch them eat or drink, hope is generated…because you hope that if they are eating, they are getting better and feeling better.

My mom would always come armed with tea and biscuits every time my heart was broken or when I was upset about one of those teenage 'why me' issues. When made with love, tea is like a magic potion. By the time you reach the end of the cup, you often feel better. A rescue friend must have sensed my need for comfort during the week as she left the most perfect home-made pie in a vets for me to pick up. With every mouthful I was transported back to a time of home baking and that familial safe feeling. I wish I had appreciated home more and the person who made where I lived a home. It reminds you how a home is more than bricks and mortar: it is the people or a person who makes it so. I think Joey ate because he really wanted to be better; he didn't feel like eating.

As I type this I'm thinking how as humans we can be so alike and so very different. Some of us will do so much to alleviate suffering and there are those who cause so much suffering – and they don't even see that it is suffering they create and maintain. Like the 13-year-old collie I saw for sale on done deal – her life now is chained in a barn. I just think of slavery when I see chains and yet people post these pictures without any shame and sometimes, we see them and accept them as normal for some animals. What is one person's wrong is another person's right; what is one person's treasure is another person's rubbish. How complex we are?

And back to apathy. I told my friend the other day how I couldn't react when another friend told me a very upsetting case involving (yet again) a pig. I think of what Pete the Vet said last week about pigs being as intelligent as dogs and treated so badly in terms of their needs not being met. What must they go through when they have the ability to process the way dogs do; what must they go through when they crave mental stimulation and yet are kept in dark sheds; when they need a dry bed and yet they are on concrete; when they need water and yet they just have a food bucket, and the only company is their own shadow and the only sound, their breath. What happens when all their needs are denied to them? What would happen us if locked in darkness for our entire lives? As I type this, I feel the emotion of anger, but my usual proactive reaction is not coming forth. I often fear neither the law nor danger when it comes to animals in need. But on this occasion, I've asked a fellow rescuer to help the pig. I'm so afraid apathy will take over. Yes, I've actually said the words, 'I can't watch it' when my friend went to show me the video of the poor pig. Usually I grab the phone and take it in, and I feel every emotion the animal suffering feels. But during the week I didn't want to feel at all. When another friend told me she hadn't seen a horse I feed in her field, I drove by the field and couldn't look in the first time I passed, because I didn't want to see that she was no longer there. Maybe this is compassion fatigue. It has been lingering for a while; perhaps it gets worse before it gets better. I'm sure it's passing. Because there are places and people I need to face again for the animals' sakes. In some cases, I think it is the people I dread facing.

Over the last few days, I've heard the new Commissioner of the Guards speak on the radio. His voice is assertive but compassionate, and he is full of understanding for 'what is' but aware of what has to change, and you get a feeling of the impact his 'mindful punch' could have. I got a chance to shake his hand during the week and I wished him well in his new position; part of me didn't want to let go until I mentioned the many times guards have dismissed their role they should play in animal welfare, and I wanted to tell him of a guard who went out of her way and changed the future of one dog I fed. When faced with a 'legal wall' as we stood facing the dog that looked at her waiting to open his gate, she thought outside the legal box of limitations to get him out of a place where he was absolutely miserable. But with an army of minders and PR people, I reluctantly let go of his hand before I started my wish list for animals in need.

Some people may not have magic wands, but they have the potential to create change for both people and animals who are suffering. Even the slightest change: a bed, a shelter, food, or maybe company can make a big difference to their daily lives. I know so many rescuers that make the impossible happen and they leave you saying, 'how did they do that?' Life is not a fairy-tale until we as people make it so. We have the power sometimes to create the 'happy ever afters' – some people have the legal powers to do so – if only they all used their authority proactively and consistently when it comes to animal welfare. And that is why it is so important we get to the AFAWI March on October the 4th – to plant the seeds for a lasting change. Without numbers, a voice for animals is a mere whisper on the state platform; with a large gathering, it becomes a roar!

Life: a series of pictures

September 27th, 2018

Today I went searching for a photo. As I spread them out on the table, what struck me was, there were no animals – not one at all! Their absence was everywhere. It triggered much reflection.

My mother often pleaded with me, 'please don't start going out too early.' But that was my goal: to get into the local nightclub at sixteen. I reached that goal. She was probably right about going out too early: you burn out too quickly. I did in my twenties. Sixteen was too young; I saw too much too soon. From practically living in them and running one, I prematurely started to dream about early nights on a Saturday night and being able to live in slippers for the weekend. How did I keep going, often sprang to mind when I finally hung up my heels?

Rescue work is like being out all the time: you want to go home but someone always gets your attention, so you stay out a bit longer. The rescue noise is constantly in your head. The sound never changes; the problems remain the same.

On October the 4th many like-minded people (animal lovers, rescuers, advocates & activists) will be brought together to attend a protest organised by Action for Animal Welfare Ireland, to highlight how the existing legislation is not being utilised to stop the animal welfare crisis in our country. The level of cruelty is certainly not reflected in media or court reports. When there is an actual prosecution, the punishment in no way reflects the crime committed. How can any judge give an 18 month ban to a farmer for nearly starving to death 40 collies whilst 3 were found dead? How can another judge wish a man well in court when he faced a serious charge of cruelty to 47 horses? Those who didn't die had to be put to sleep.

During the week My Lovely Horse Rescue, Cork lost a three-month-old foal called Freda. Just a baby but found for sale at a fair. She fought to live; she tried everything to hold on. Maybe, even as a baby; she knew this was a life worth living for. Her owners stole this life from her before she was even born. Her tiny body savaged by human neglect. Freda was just a baby, but her death never made the paper even though humans caused her death. It is akin to murder as are all the other cases of animal abuse that lead to death. Why is the suffering of an animal less than our suffering? As difficult as it is, we must hold on to the picture of Freda and any other animals who suffered terribly. If we don't remember them, their deaths are truly in vain. Their tragic life picture should move us enough to keep reporting and keep fighting for change.

Yes, many photos will be taken at the protest; I hope when we look back at these images, we will say, the fight and demands for change; the refusal to accept the indifference; the reporting and highlighting was all worth it. Those responsible to protect the welfare of this country's animals will finally do their job. Only then will we be finally able to go home.

And back to photos …. they reflect our way of being and looking at any given time. They show us what mattered to us; they show us who mattered. They show us growing. They make us reminisce. Sometimes I find myself looking for certain pictures in my phone: mainly the 'before rescue' and 'after rescue' photos. These are the pictures that I will grow old looking at – especially the ones where the horses went from being tethered to green fields. Where their bodies went from skeletal to perfect condition. Where their hanging heads became proud again.

Yes, a picture certainly speaks a thousand words. A picture of an animal in need screams many more.

Say something: we're giving up on you

October 7th, 2018

Behind every picture is a context and some people don't want to know it. Especially so if there is an ugly truth that speaks the thousand words.

The last week clearly illustrated two opposing views on animals and their rights. Ballinasloe Fair demonstrated the callous and apathetic mindset that lies at the core of animal abuse. It illustrates vividly the people who contribute to animal cruelty and who allow it to continue. Ballinasloe has no problem with hosting people who neglect animals in their own backyard whilst local authorities and officials removed a few token cases of neglect. What about the ones left behind? The 'given up' eyes that stared out of crates; the dehydrated and hungry animals that were in public view. What makes these people think it's OK to stand alongside these animals at an event attended by over 100,000 people? The words are 'no legal consequences' and 'no public shame'.

Luckily there are those amongst us who will stand outside Leinster House and will shout the words: 'there is no excuse for animal abuse'; there are diverse members of society willing to hold signs that scream the obvious words 'enforce the law'. And behind the tired pleading voices are the 'hard to look at' images of the animals we know of. We have woken to their tragic endings on Facebook and we have gone to bed with the 'if only'. The 'if onlys' if the relevant legislation was simply enforced. After all isn't the law in place to maintain a civilised society?

There is nothing civilised about Ballinasloe Fair. What is civilised or normal about emaciated puppies kept in basins that belong in a kitchen sink. Bright orange basins with rusty metal caging keeping them caged within. What is civilised about a clearly distressed foal holding the weight of a young man who has no regard for her underdeveloped frame? Her top line akin to a half moon; her lame legs buckling under his weight; her eyes bulging with fear. She probably knows nothing else.

There is a committee that stand over this fair; there is a county council that turn a blind eye; there is a huge sector of the public that are OK with this. And then there is our President: our mindful, poetic, animal loving President opening this fair; a fair that broke many an animal lover's heart this week. What are we seeing that he failed to see? Surely his PR machine would have done the public relations check on such an event and foresaw from previous fairs that it was an event he should have steered away from. Perhaps our President should have used the opportunity to say why he would not attend the fair. And the reasons why he should not have attended were aplenty outside Leinster House on October the 4th at the AFAWI protest calling for the consistent enforcement of the existing Animal Welfare Legislation. This protest demonstrated that amongst animal lovers and rescuers is an informed and rational voice. The rational voice our society is hungry for. Abuse of the vulnerable amongst us cannot be tolerated. The rational voice does not accept legal jargon and token legislation; it calls for enforcement. The rational voice that asks why would the state pay lucrative and secure salaries to authorised welfare officers and vets who aren't doing their jobs consistently when such blatant breach of their job remit costs the state not just financially but society starts to break down when we allow abuse to continue. Animal abuse is not just about animals: it is diagnostic criteria for other abuses and crimes. Further abuses and crimes that seriously hurt and kill people.

The health of a nation can be judged by how it treats its animals. It does not say a lot when our President can love and adore his Bernese dogs, but he is OK for other dogs to be crammed into crates and to be put up for sale with no access to food or water.

In years to come future generations will ask us 'how could we let this happen?' And I will be without guilt when I say, I stood with compassionate and informed people on October the 4th who asked the Minister of Agriculture to stop the animal welfare crisis in Ireland. A crisis that is becoming part of the very fabric of who we now are as a nation. Brave are the people who take on the battle that is the animal welfare issue. Selfless are the people who take on a cause with no financial or personal gain. Brave and Selfless is what the world needs more of.

The pain that has no cure

October 17th, 2018

Seventeen years ago, someone I loved so very much died. Before she died, she cried that she was not ready to go. Some people are; she wasn't, and so she fought an uphill battle to live until she could no more. Her reason to live were the people she loved.

As far back as I can remember I use to imagine – really imagine people I loved dying so I could see how bad the pain would be. From a young age I couldn't stand hearing about any type of ending and this spilled into my teens and then into adulthood. I guess nobody is ever ready or able but when you find yourself crying at airport departures for people who you don't even know their names …. well you have to pull yourself together! It's a full-time job for me.

There is a funny story to one of my teary moments watching airport good-byes, but I will save that for another post. I also could never end a relationship! No matter how bad it was, the thoughts of an ending made it easier to stay. How lucky I was that my boyfriends in my twenties didn't quiet feel the same about endings.

How do I cope with this ending phobia? I simply block it, when it comes into my head, and I literally shake it off. However, animal rescue makes me face my worst fears frequently. Yes, I face them, I feel the feelings and I literally crumble inside, but I maintain that face of composure that comes with practice. Whether it's a rescue dying or a rehoming – endings are plentiful. They are dreadful – even the happy ones!

Today was one of those days. Prince Harry, a beautiful, loving, and gentle kitten is dying on me. I took him out of SCAR one Sunday, months ago, after I had finished cleaning the cat cabin. I remember asking my friend Linda could she reach up for him as he was perched on a beam in his run. I'm not too good with feral cats and she reached up and brought him into her arms. He wasn't feral; he wasn't well, so I brought him home. The lady who owns the rescue wanted him to get more attention also.

And this is how his short little life has panned out: fighting one thing after the other. To find out that a six-month-old has gone suddenly blind and unable to stand is heart-breaking. He can't tell you if he is hurting; he can't tell you what would make it better. Many vets and one specialist later, he has been diagnosed with FIP and the words 'there is no cure' become like a verbal boomerang: returning again and again with the same finality punch. He purrs constantly even though he can't see or walk. And if he had words, I think he would say, 'I want to live a bit longer'. The cats here adore him and lately sometimes you see one at each side of him, to hold him up. They know and they are doing what they can. I'm thinking about his ending before it's begun. Every vet visit, I thought it was the last. Every day he had to take medication; I said it's not forever. Every time he pushes his head against mine, I told him how much I loved him. I thought he would be the cat who would be with me as I cross various milestones. I thought he was my forever cat when a home let him down as a kitten.

Animals suffer so much in this world and you wonder how they make sense of it with no words. They feel but they can't verbalise their feelings. How blessed we are that most of us are gifted to have the ability to express, to share and to name our emotions. We need to do it more! Animals are so very vulnerable: they are without a voice.

Today I returned to a place where a friend and I had put up a dog run for two puppies. I wanted to fill it with toys and water and food bowls. Every toy I laid down the two puppies quickly ran with them into their new house my friend built for them. They distracted me from my broken heart as did a little boy who lives here. It was as if he knew, as he ran to fill the water bowls, and fixed the run up. He asked me lots of questions and I enjoyed answering them. His only request was that I find a Santa Teddy for the puppies. Our first encounter wasn't as smooth. From today, it can only get better. Leaving this site is made easier knowing that the puppies here have an insulated dog box and a run to keep them off the road. Little things to delay their ending and to make their lives nicer.

The little boy's mother asked me as I was leaving 'was I religious that I loved animals so much?' I smiled and looked at the beautiful baby she held in her arms. 'I love them as much as you love your baby,' I replied. And I do. Animals are forever children that need and deserve the same protection every child has and should have. Loving them is a good start. How could you not?

There is no cure for grief but as an elderly man from Connemara said to me, 'you'll learn to walk on again without them; you just might go through your remaining years with a limp.'

My Prince Charming

October 26th, 2018

On Wednesday I couldn't leave the house for long and Frank kindly dropped haylage to my door. Before he left, he asked me why did I think my little rescue, Prince Harry, was different from the rest I've lost? Sometimes we have to ponder on questions that require some kind of reasoning, but I didn't have to think about the answer. Because I thought I would grow old with my Prince Harry. For those of us who really let animals into our lives, we don't just think of growing old with our partners. We think of the other loves in our lives that have four paws that etch deep into our hearts and minds. Is it because they are forever 'child like'? Full of hope and enthusiasm. They fully depend on us and in return they love us consistently regardless of our bad days and 'bad hair' days! Maybe we should look more at animals' and what they do for us – it is not an effort, it's innate in them – to be there for us as much as they can. Are they the role models we should look up to? Are they the last remaining signposts to humanity?

Any animal that crosses my path, I care for and yes, I show them love as if they were my own. It's not a choice; it is like leaves to trees. But along comes 'one' and it's like you have lived a lifetime with them. I guess when an animal battles illness again and again, you bond very quickly. Just as humans do when they share on an emotional level or as a carer. It is that attachment that is way harder to unhook from, unlike physical attraction. So, it's a hidden dating tip! Share deeply! There will be more dates then! There was an actual experiment that set out to prove this theory. Twenty-four people who never met were paired up in a room. Half were told they could only talk on a superficial level whilst the remaining half were to share on an emotional level. The latter couples ended up becoming actual couples.

Prince Harry had FIP which instils fear into cat lovers! I heard the letters and did not know what they meant. I learned so quickly from two vets and research on-line pushed me from one site to the other – I desperately wanted a site that would not use the word 'fatal'.

Part of me thinks – maybe the child in me – still believes if I love enough and pray enough – I can make animals and yes, people I love better. That along with alternative cures. It hasn't worked this time. Prince Harry has left this world. Our last night together, I cherished his smell, his softness and his tiny pink nose that pushed into my cheek to make sure I knew how much he loves me and to tell me, 'I'm still here'. The head bumps and nose kisses weakened as his body started to shut down over the last few days.

FIP is hard to diagnose and nearly impossible to treat. At the vets he captured many hearts and I'm so grateful to Ennis Veterinary Clinic for their genuine care for him. And for guiding me to a decision that I'm a coward to face. Yesterday one by one, the nurses said goodbye to a prince that lived before: such was his human-like traits. He loved candles and Lyric FM. It will be our connection now for the rest of my days.

Cats get a raw deal. A lot of people dislike them. So many live homeless as feral cats and depend on someone leaving out a bit for them to eat or they depend on their hunting skills (9 out of 10 hunts fail). They need rescues to trap them, to neuter them, to save them from a lifetime of fights or having babies. They are incredibly loving animals when given any kind of care. Neutering cats would end so much suffering. Why can't more people do the decent thing? Why do so many intentionally hurt them?

Another thing occurred to me earlier. How we can send texts to people when we are angry or 'in giving out' mode, not mindful of what they might be dealing with as they read the 'verbal punch'. Wednesday, as I cradled Harry, I read a message on my phone. Another rescuer giving out to me in the harshest way possible. No, they didn't know. But I told them. It changed nothing.

Prince Harry at six months old was just a baby. Someone didn't neuter his mommy, and someone dictated his fate as a kitten born to a feral/homeless mother. Just like the six-month-old foal with a furry tail rescued by HHO, just a baby, a baby wearing shoes, when he should have been still with his mother being nursed. What kind of person gets up on a baby? What kind of person rolls down a window in a moving car and throws kittens out on the road? Who are you and what is wrong with you? Fix it! I'm forever grateful that I got to care for this little man. It is truly a privilege but a heart-breaking one.

I decided I would go to Dublin to the Blog Awards and win it for him and all the animals let down by humans. Unfortunately, I came home with being a finalist, with no award. But I will take that. That is what I got, and that in itself is a gift to the animals and recognition of them. That will do – for this year.

Doing the maths

November 5th, 2018

I was never one for numbers. There is a real possibility I have dyscalculia, but I wasn't privileged with that 'get me out of trouble' diagnoses when I was constantly sent to the board to complete maths problems in school. Yes, setting someone up for a downfall comes to mind but I'm sure I gave the others in my class a sense of 'feeling better about their ability'. I had none. The board work did not cure my disability much to my teacher's frustration nor did a ruler across my hands.

Roll on a few decades, there are certain numbers I can read when they come in the form of statistics and when there is an emotional attachment to them. To read the latest equine seizure statistics from Clare leaves me with a sense of outrage coupled with 'is this a joke?' It's hard to celebrate the unrealistically low figures like 18 horses seized in 2017 and even less for this year so far. Because behind these low figures are all the horses that died in fields from hunger, or untreated illnesses, and in one case, after being attacked by dogs – all horses that should have been seized! What about all the horses starving right now that won't make the 2018 figures and who should be seized? What about all the horses taken in by rescues after being reported to the council or the department? All the horses let down by the same bodies. So, the latest statistics are no realistic reflection of the state of equine welfare in Clare. They scream 'seizure tokenism'.

This morning I read a notice on a fence issued by the department. A notice placed after many concerning calls to the department for two mares and a foal in a field with nothing to eat. The notice asked the owners to provide feed & water and outlined what would happen if they didn't. Did the official who cable-tied the notice not take into consideration the emaciated foal or her mother with her ribs protruding and a belly full of worms. Did the official scan for chips? Did they check for an equine number? He would have got close enough as these horses are so starved of attention that they are so overly interested and affectionate when someone stops off at their fence. Yes, hay arrived today but not hay a starving horse would be grateful for. They should be part of the 2018 seizure statistics; they won't be.

I'm sure the statistics for pounds nationwide are also a source of much upset for dog lovers and related rescuers. Especially the numbers PTS. Behind all of these statistics are human faces and behaviour that is far removed from normative or mindful of animal needs. Behind these figures are the dogs who never made the cut when it came to being rehomed, or when it came to being assessed for rehoming. They unfortunately became part of statistics. Their names, their personalities, their stories reduced to a number.

So when you have local public figures jumping on a celebratory bandwagon to fly the flag of low seizure numbers or low PTS statistics, you want to take them from their 'head in the clouds' pedestal and put them in a field with a sick mare who is feeding a foal, and tell them how her owners won't get the vet for her. How somebody hand feeds her to make sure she is getting some sort of nutrition. You want them to look at the empty water buckets that are filled by people who are not their owners and you want them to speak to the landowner who has not given permission for their land to be used. You want them to drive into certain areas where horses lives are limited by a few feet of rope, where they are sustained by the grass beneath them, and are at the mercy of those who own them to untie them and move them to a new patch every day. You want them to visit pounds unannounced and see the fear behind closed doors; fear that could be alleviated by a simple thing called 'care'.

What hope is there to reduce the number of dogs seeking homes when county councils award licenses to puppy farms to keep breeding – the same breeders who do not provide the basics for their breeding bitches and dogs kept under lock and key. What hope is there when the law of the land for animal welfare is not consistently enforced when it is broken? Law enforcement should not be 'pick and miss'. Why should the same laws be applied differently when the animal welfare issue is the same?

The only hope left in this country for most animals let down by humans are rescuers. Rescue: the only light in this dismally dark animal welfare tunnel. The keeper of the light and power is a minister who fails to see the darkness. Maybe it's time rescues guided him through it until he has his moment of enlightenment. Until that happens, he stands over a law that is as futile as an empty bucket for a dehydrated horse.

The gift of 'no' with a big red bow

November 29th, 2018

It's that time of year again! Unless you buy into the 'keep it simple season', Christmas – well the commercial option, is not for the faint hearted. And for those of us whose hearts are constantly torn between the animal and human world, the puppy buying season leaves us like Christmas grim reapers. We are not very jolly and the sight of a puppy with a festive, present bow ignites an array of complex and strong emotions that would knock McGregor out. Think more 'NO NO NO' than 'HO HO HO' that packs our mental punches!

It's a pity we can't instil the fear of anything in those buying from breeders for Christmas. There is no stopping some, but we can keep trying. Trying is key! But can anyone shed light on the type of mind that can navigate their way past all the 'Adopt Don't Shop!' campaigns. Selfish Stubbornness comes to mind – the kind of mentality that screams 'no one tells me what to do'!

As a CBT Counsellor I get to work with teenagers. It's both a privilege and a source of frustration. The teenager is often not the problem: it's the adult or adults in their lives that should be sitting in the counselling chair, and then there is that big problem that originates from a small word called 'NO'. What is it with this one word that can cause 'worlds' to come crashing down? This need to get 'now' or 'what I want' with no excuses allowed has created deeply unhappy young people! I've seen polite and placid teenagers transform into selfish and insatiable beings who refuse point blank to accept 'NO' to any of their demands. This aggressive reaction creates another reaction in those who have to live with such behaviour and the reaction is usually 'OK so'! Give up and give in comes to mind. And hey presto begins a lifetime of 'me me me' and trust me that causes a lot of mental health problems too!

So, when it comes to your child wanting a puppy for Christmas, switch into rational, assertive adult and say 'NO'. Because it is often the case when you say NO to someone, you are saying YES to yourself – whilst teaching the young person in your life that we often have to wait for what we want or sometimes we can't always get it. Besides, Christmas might not be a good time to introduce a new pet into a house.

I know a woman who made her children walk rescue dogs every weekend for a year before she gave into getting them a dog. They proved their interest and compassion for dogs and a year later they adopted their family pet.

'No' is the gift that lasts a lifetime when you plant the word early in a young mind. I'm glad my beautiful and giving mother said 'NO' a lot!! She even recycled our Christmas presents and how right she was! We never knew the difference really. But as they say, 'don't try this at home'! Today's kids might just have a wee problem with that!! Perhaps getting one of those plastic small televisions that played 'Old McDonald had a farm' on loop possibly contributed to my need to save animals. Afterall I did get it for two Christmases in a row.

Learning lessons in love

December 14th, 2018

The last seven days thought me many lessons. We truly are students of life. The quicker we learn the lessons, the less likely we are to get stuck in the same problems again and again! I am not always the quickest to learn: the solution could be right in front of me, but I can even question the right answer.

I was so proud of myself Sunday. I got all the dogs walked, cats sorted, horses fed and car ready for a road trip to Cork. I'm a bad timekeeper (usually) so I was really chuffed I was going to be on time to pay a visit to Rose & Bear. Approaching Charleville, the oncoming traffic was heavy heading to the Munster Match. The sun hit the road leaving a sudden glare and amidst the hazy glow was a silhouette of a woman standing in the middle of busy traffic with a dog. After pulling over we quickly learned the dog had been hit and couldn't walk and lifting her caused much stress. Ciara had decided to stand with her as she was more noticeable than a solitary dog on the road. Her fear was, she would be hit again. As we stood with her, cars indicated to drive around us – some flying by and one lady bore the ugliest of faces: scowling, impatient, intolerant as she peered down from her SUV.

I went back to my car to get a blanket to roll the dog onto and after realizing her home was right beside us, we carried her home.

Through the front door, down the hall, and into a family kitchen. Four strangers and their dog. All the poor dog wanted to do was get to his upset owner. She couldn't walk. So, a call was made to a vet. Jessie was lifted into the owner's van and the plan was we would follow him to the vets. Except my car was locked with the keys inside. Nobody ever told me a car can mind itself by locking itself. Lovely thought except when the keys are in there. One broken window later, we were back on the road again. It was one cold drive. But if you don't inject humour into it, it will inject a lot of bad humour into the day. Main thing: Jessie was alive. And so, for a few hours, everything is OK again, you have a lovely visit, and you head home. The second we pulled in, the words 'ring me, it's urgent!' flashes up on your screen.

Fifteen minutes later, you're in a small estate going from door to door, to ask them about a foal down in a field beside them. They aren't in a position to help at first until one of the younger men brings a horse blanket to keep her tiny body off the wet ground. You leave with the words: 'she is not to be put down'. And so, begins the emotional tug of war. Your innate reaction is to do anything to keep a baby girl alive versus wanting her to die. I met this foal before; I fed her in another location, but I was told she had been sold when I enquired where she was gone?

The day I met Ciara, I knew her time here would be short. She was ghostly angelic; she did not belong here. I asked my

112

friend to put pressure on the department vet to visit her, her mum, and another pony. Another two ladies had also persisted with calls. And there was a department visit and a notice to feed went up. No urgent intervention for an emaciated mare in foal with her own foal by her side. They were eating the bark off the trees that enclosed this field at the side of a busy road. Ciara ate tiny amounts. Some days I thought she was turning a corner and then the owners moved her to nothingness. Here is where I discovered the truth: as I stood in a bleak field on my knees, with my hands holding her beautiful face. The tug of war was won. I lost

On Monday after getting all the hay out, a call comes in that there is a pony with an injured leg in another area. It's dark, and a tiny wet Shetland is tied to a pallet with a cut to his back-right leg. I had the vet out to him a few months ago. So many rescuers give me bits from time to time that make up a first aid box. So wound wash and Botanica seem to have sorted this wound. The kids here are great, and it is them who take care of the horses, but kids don't have resources. We untied the pony and walked around trying to find any sheltered spot. And so, it was back to a corner where another tiny rescue pony called Little Leo once lived. I said to the kids, I was looking forward to my Christmas present from them. One of them asked, 'what do you want, Catriona?' I replied, 'something girlie!' He made me laugh when he looked puzzled and turned to the other boys, 'what's that?' he asked.

I spent the last month worrying about an up-coming

appointment. When you're sitting in a waiting room with other ladies all thinking probably the same, 'what if?' It really reminds you how living fully every day is so important. Something I should remind myself of more. Every day is one little life that we are not guaranteed tomorrow. Facing this was made a lot easier with someone who has promised me whatever happens, the horses will be fed. Thank God, I was back feeding that night. I have spent the week trying to get owners to feed their horses. Some horses I don't feed anymore. I can't. Some have died since.

It really tests me when people make throw away comments like 'they don't feed them because you are!' Let me tell you, some don't care if their horses are fed or not because there are plenty where they came from. When I first started feeding, it was because of dead horses in certain areas, and numerous unanswered calls and emails to the council and the welfare section of the department for an intervention.

Right now, I'm holding some horses onto life with this great hope that one day they will be seized or rescued. I'm giving relief from the awful pain that comes from hunger. Official visits and reviews do not keep horses alive as they wait for someone in an office to sign a notice to feed them or seize them. I remember one time there was a threat to seize horses I was feeding but that is all it was. A threat! Seizures aren't necessary when there are pending surrenders, and there are some that get lucky enough when their owners decide to let them go. Letting go of an animal to a better life is the kindest thing to do when all you have to offer them is nothing.

What is really going on?

This week I took a call from a man missing his two dogs. He had formed an ill-informed opinion based on someone's well thought-out 'opinion'. Well-thought-out based on biases and on another's need to create trouble. So according to the owner the dogs could only have been taken by people who had a lot of experience handling dogs and they often send dogs abroad. He proceeded to tell me he had it narrowed down to a number of rescue people. So, I listened and told him that no one stole his dogs and the rest I kept to myself. The rest being: nobody in any position of authority should plant seeds especially when those seeds take root and grow into reactive emotions. But the person who handed him the seeds had a clear agenda, I guess. How dangerous some agendas can be? This put rescuers in a very dangerous position with this man.

It's not just the rescue world that is laced with hidden agendas, rivalry, back-stabbing and corruption. It exists in many charities and companies. But the problem is all those nasty things don't sit well amidst causes for care and welfare. It's quite ironic to be saving animals whilst pushing others to the edge with torment. Yes, it's happening. It's so terribly damaging.

Sunday started with the usual pre-transport anxiety. There were three ponies and two goats from two different locations to be brought to South Tipperary. A partition was made to separate them and the usual 'just in case' tricks packed. Everything went so smoothly apart from google maps reminding us what a circle is – again and again. Yes, we were going around in circles as we got closer to our destination. And then nothing prepared me for what happened next.

In the yard I was introduced to a rescuer. The name automatically triggered a flashback of tags and screen shots. And so, I got my chance. My chance to ask, 'How could you write that stuff about me when you don't even know me?' She wore a smirk which was quite consoling: how can you expect anything else from someone who can't say the word 'sorry'. So, her facial expression made me care less about what she said about me. Back in August, whilst I was caring for a kitten subjected to a night of terror, she was posting nasty comments based on my posts about the kitten and then came the long lists of 'what she would have done!' No regard for the rescuers involved in a very complex case.

Sometimes blocking works: blocking all the character assassinations. If you didn't, you probably would give up – give up the helping and caring – the very acts that we, as rescuers, share in common. What's really going on is privy to each of us when we act cruelly or irrationally. I'm not sure what's really going on for people who take pleasure in being unfairly cruel. All I know is that I've worked with people who weren't able to block or weren't as resilient. And they are no longer here today. None of us know the limits of the people we cross paths with. 2019 has already seen many horrific cruelty cases come to the attention of rescues – not even a month into a new year. If you were to only look at the world through the eyes of a rescued animal, you might just want to run for the hills.

But there are many stories that throw a big life buoy around the rescuer's deflating spirit. There is a springer that has lived her life chained in a back yard. Her adorable belly crawl is due to a broken leg left to heal with no medical attention. Heart-breaking to watch. Tomorrow, Baby Dog rescue will be bringing her back to Clare to begin again. Now they are the tales I can live with.

When love is not enough

February 14th, 2019

There is something inadequate about this tiny word 'love'. It's like it's missing half of itself sometimes: in certain circumstances and when it's used as a defence by certain people to cover up their bad behaviour – 'but I love . . .' But one thing for certain: there is nothing certain about love in the rescue world.

Today someone told me they loved their animals. I thought to myself that he must have been devoid of my idea of love if he thought he loved his emaciated horses. Love alone cannot feed or do the job of a vet. Then there are those who love money so much that they will deny their money-making animals any sense of being looked after. Then when you love animals completely as equals to us you are ridiculed by many people even more than those who stand before our courts for cruelty to animals. Yes, some people sneer at the heart of a rescuer, a heart that drives rescuers on to save, to rehabilitate, and to rehome animals broken by humans. It is love at its best: when you love unconditionally and when you are no longer at the centre. It is selfless and it is pure and it's what the world needs now.

Last week I came under so much fire for looking for a lost rescue. And yes, I wish I was exaggerating. It nearly broke me. My mind and its makeup can't comprehend intentional hurt or punishment when no crime was committed. It is the absolute driving hunger to make safe again that had me wet and cold for days going through the same fields again and again. A rescue had lost a dog who was terrified of humans. They seemed to want to cover it up by not looking for him. Imagine. And when he was found and brought to the home intended for him, the personal attacks at times became too much. How does a rational mind comprehend someone being so angry for doing the right and kindest thing?

I know I'm slowing losing many people from my life because maybe I do love animals more than most. Maybe a lot of us do, and I don't need to list the reasons why that might be the case. I do know this, that one animal in your life can remedy so much emotional pain. One animal in your life can give you purpose and take away loneliness. One animal in our lives is possibly the best executioner of much human pain. I know many people who would vouch for this. I've thrown a lifeline to a young man at risk of ending his life. The lifeline was a bouncy Labrador. He is alive and a father today. This beautiful golden boy loved my client so much, he started to love himself again.

Yes, I'm guilty of loving animals more than some humans but that is one crime that does not deserve any punishment. The punishment belongs to those who purposely harm or kill animals.

If only the misdirected and misleading rescue ridicule was rerouted to animal abusers. They might just fear public wrath so much that it could become a deterrent to abuse.

Love might never be enough for us until we sort out our issues that keep denting it and changing it; even keeping it from our door but for animals their only currency is simply love. They let nothing get in the way of showing it – unless they are afraid. We need to learn from their way of being which is simply being as they are – without agenda. And that should be enough.

This Valentine's I hope you know the love of good humans or animals or even both.

To Whom It May Concern

February 27th, 2019

I visited your dog! You know, the one you loved so much but sold away. I thought you might like to know how she is doing in the home you never checked before you handed her over to a stranger. You see, it's not a home. Her space is a few feet, tied to a fence. She lies on muck and stones. No, this isn't the home she is used to. Is it? I know this because I was told. You see she never stops crying for you. Every day she waits for you to take her home. The man, you know the one, the stranger you sold the dog you loved to, he told me you always had her with you. He told me she isn't used to being outdoors. At least he was honest!

You know I hear her every day. Even when I'm not beside her. Fields away she can be heard. She probably hopes you'll hear her too. But you're far away. It is hard not to be upset. I bought her a chain. Yes, I bought a chain for the dog you loved so much. I never did that before. The rope was choking her, and her legs were being wound up in a thick ravelling rope. We gave her a house and a bed. She never ripped it up like the other dogs here do. Because she knows what a bed is. You gave the dog you loved everything she needed. I'm sure many people complimented your dog you loved so much. I wonder when people ask you where she is, what do you say? Hardly, 'I sold her away!'

She's so beautiful and soulful. She puts her paw on my knee as if to say, please take me home but I can't because you sold her away. The dog you loved so much has food, toys, a small wooden hut because I love the dog you loved so much. She has everything but a home and happiness – therefore nothing really. The dog you loved so much has a broken heart.

Why didn't you surrender her to a rescue rather than surrender her fate to the cruel deal, that is Done Deal. Done Deal don't do happy-ever-afters for animals; they never claim to. A rescue would have checked every possible home until they found the best one. But I guess you put a price on the dog you loved so much.

She will spend the next few weeks waiting for you until the day comes when she gives up and gives into life on a chain without you.

Wish you were here for her. I don't know where you are but maybe someone will get this letter to you.

From a stranger who loves the dog you once loved so much!

The Sensitive Warriors

March 18th, 2019

How many times has someone said to you? You're over sensitive when it comes to animals. How many times have people told you to stop being so sensitive? Stopping yourself from being sensitive, is akin to trying to change your eye colour! Nope, funny that, no matter how many times you're told not to be, it just stays the bloody same. A bottle of wine helps and sleep too! I'm waiting to see how Rhodiola works out. Many rescuers have recommended it. Yes, seemingly it calms that sensitive beast within!

Doesn't the world need sensitive people. Highly sensitive people are empathetic. If you have empathy for another being's struggle or suffering, you will move mountains for them. 'I' becomes the instrument of change for 'them'. They get us out of our often self-defeating, selfish, obsessive, monkey minds! It's a win-win. I constantly say this: having a self-less purpose not only enriches our lives but it is a remedy for much mental conflict. Staying in our own heads is just the same as living in a dark cave for some. And in this type of darkness the light will never break through unless we find a way out. The signpost reads: purpose, care, giving, and helping others. It is a real pity more of us don't follow it – for our own sakes. Lasting friendships and relationships also grow in the fertile garden that is charity or volunteering. And we all need more of them.

Before I got into rescuing, I can say I went through approximately twenty outfit changes some days. I was consumed with 'nothing being good enough' and the goal posts constantly moved from one 'must have purchase' to another, to fulfil a hungry part of me that was never satisfied. It turns out I was feeding that part the wrong diet all along and a bigger hunger was being created. One called 'what is the point?' The constant search in shops and lifestyle was futile. Rescuing animals is not for everyone. But there are many other types of rescuing. And when we reach out to help others, we are helping ourselves.

Today, I was consumed by self-pity. I had an MRI on Thursday. When I went in, the nurse prepping me wasn't the nicest. When she brought me back to the changing room after the scan, she was suddenly kind and empathetic. That worried me more, so I asked her, what did you see? And she smiled, 'it's pretty big, Catriona, but the radiologist will read it!' Yes, today I was consumed with fear, self-pity and the worry about what happens next. Another argument which stemmed from being overly sensitive didn't help either. In fact, it hurts terribly. Yes HSPs (highly sensitive people) are not the easiest to be with. But it's not a choice nor is it an illness.

So today I climbed out of my 'pity cave' and I went to Pet Stop. I bought haylage and drove to the motorway ponies that deserve to feel sorry for themselves. Their lives are bleak, their field is flooded, and they are very hungry. It's not the easiest task cutting open haylage on a motorway. You have to keep a good grip on the plastic wrapping to ensure it doesn't land on a passing window-screen. Out of my 'bouncing back' came 'bellies less hungry'.

And then you get back into your car, turn on the radio and hear about a mum of three that will never go home; you hear about three teenagers crushed queuing for a disco who will never say the words Mommy or Daddy again. Then you realise whether you are highly sensitive or not, you are blessed with being alive today. It's important to have gratitude for that.

The kind of kindness

April 6th, 2019

Many people over the last few hours watched (on various social media platforms) a baby kangaroo holding up her paw peacefully as she faced a group of aggressive teenagers. Yet again, these hard to watch clips, remind us that we need to proactively and intensely teach kindness as we would any other key skill from a young age. It is neither innate nor guaranteed. It is now a necessity if we are going to salvage morality and humanity. We need to show, demonstrate, and practice it. How many times will a parent or teacher say, 'show me how you've been kind today!' as much as they would say 'show me your homework'. You see, when we ask ourselves, 'what has happened to this world when we see or hear of terrible acts of cruelty?' The answer is 'kindness has left the minds and hands of many'. What has replaced it, is of great concern.

The 'buzz' or 'need fulfilment' that some people get from abusing someone or an animal is very short-lived. I wish they could for once experience 'the high' or 'the self-satisfaction' from being kind. But you can't strip someone of a way of life and leave nothing in its place. You need to show another way of being.

I am quite fiery and get so angry when I see an animal being abused. I learnt that I am no good to them if I let anger immobilise me. Anger burns bridges: you can't engage with owners or authorities from an angry platform. Yes, I'm in danger of becoming less kind because of my frustration (ironically) over the lack of kindness in the world. But I'm mindful, and I'm in restoration mode.

There was a time I spent about five mornings a week in an area where there were animals – all in need of help. It took everything in me to drive in, to open the door, to get out what I needed from the boot, and walk by the residents dotted here and there – not knowing when I would be told to stop coming in. Some talked to me, some didn't, but no adult helped. The kids did. There was a day I simply lost it, some of them were running a lame pony, others instilling fear in another, and the water buckets were empty, even though a deal was made to keep them full. Yes, I was expecting a lot from children, but there was no hope of the adults doing it. So, I gave out and I tried to make them see what it would be like for them. It didn't work. I knew that as I looked from face to face. So, I pulled back before it was too late. I grabbed a bucket and filled it with feed, and I walked up to one of the poorly ponies. She walked over with hesitation. One by one, my little friends followed. And I passed the bucket to the one whose only way of communicating with horses was to shout. I gave him the bucket and I asked him to talk nicely to the pony and just leave his little hand wherever the pony was OK with. I took a deep breath as I saw these tiny hands showing momentary kindness.

I can't go into this area anymore. But it means the world to me that one of these little boys visits a vet close to them from time to time, to ask for me. He is eleven and no matter how many times I told them, I wasn't a vet, they still believed I was.

Kindness is powerful: it can soothe pain; it can eradicate terrible memories; it is the seed of love for life and all living things. Without it, we will continue to see the abuse we can barely look at or read on Facebook. Demonstrating kindness is like throwing a big rock into a pond: there is a ripple effect. We need to keep throwing it out there. Kindness can suffocate: suffocate all that is hurting within us and outside of us.

Ironically, it is in the rescue world that I have witnessed pure and powerful kindness. A world where there is nothing but heartbreak. Kindness from friends seems to be the fuel that keeps tired minds and bodies going and unites us for a common cause: that all animals will know care and compassion.

Please teach the children in your life kindness. If they are kind to themselves first, they will be kind to those that cross their path. That's the kind of kindness we need: the type that starts within us.

Fill my shoes

September, 2nd, 2019

Sometimes motivation comes from remembering what you have achieved so far! And so, I sat outside and looked at my four miniature rescue ponies. Their big brown eyes were focused on my pockets – where their treats come from! All of these smallies have survived horrific abuse. They have a shared background and a shared rescue beginning. It was a dream come true for me: to get them all to safety. And so, I cried. Happy for them. One tear chased the other down my cheeks. I hope they have forgotten their past horrid life.

Temple Grandin says we can erase fear memory in horses by replacing what triggers the fear with another memory. Peaches, one of the smallies, once cowered when a hand was raised, so we started putting a treat in our hands as we got closer to him. He stopped associating a hand with pain but with a treat.

After surgery, and the removal of my 'tennis-ball' tumour, I was told, 'no more stress'. Ignoring what I see as generic medical advice, I recently visited a spiritual healer who greeted me with the line 'give it up or you're done!' She didn't know me, but she seemed to know everything my life was made up of. She had no tolerance for my disputes that started with 'But…But, I can't, But how do I stop?'

Ironically, a loose pony appeared outside her front door as I walked in. I looked at her and politely pleaded, 'can we help her first?' but her non-verbal response put me firmly on her couch. I think most of us laugh off these types of coincidences. But what if they are real signs sent to us? I have had many of them, but I shrug them of as 'isn't that mad?' kind of reaction.

Yesterday the same pre-surgery pain was back, except now on my sole ovary. And her words ricocheted around my mind. Yes, I had reduced my rescuing and the amount of hungry horses I feed. But I was still buying haylage, filling bottles of water, and loving visiting a smaller number of 'not my horses'. Alive for another day, but alive for owners who can't even fill a bucket of water for 'their horses'. You see, I don't know who will do it after me where I live. I know lots of amazing rescuers; I just don't know anyone following in their footsteps. Filling our shoes is probably not what a lot of dreams are made of.

Yes, I'm definitely doing less; I've lost my nerve and I'm thinking more of the warnings I have gotten from different owners. Yes, they cross my mind but hooves still cross there too. I used to walk into places with hay bags on my back, carrying bottles of water that I once would drive by quickly. I had numbers in my phone and when they flashed on my screen, I had to take deep breaths before answering. I don't go in anymore and I don't pick up anymore. I still feed, only from the roadside. I still face the same questions from curious passers-by, 'are they yours?' When I reply 'no', the next questions quickly follow, 'who pays for it?' and finally 'why do you feed them?' I want to say, 'why not?' Lately I let them vent, and I save my replies from minds that would never comprehend the honest answer to 'why?'

So, how would you sell the unpaid job of a rescuer? Firstly, it gets you out of your own head, and therefore silences the self-consuming thoughts that can often torment us. When you're holding a hungry or injured animal in your arms, probably the only arms that have ever offered them comfort, there is no head space for 'I' or 'me'. They hold you in the present; their presence imprints on your mind-space and ironically makes it a better place. But I'm not sure if 'making a difference' or 'unconditional' love sells it. It's not the kind of position one gets paid for retweets or shares. The love is far removed from the 'Love Island' variety. But with the stress of rescuing comes an indescribable sense of purpose and meaning. Seeing new beginnings unfold before you are life enriching. A life enriched by the fact 'I made a difference!' Is that what we want to believe when we take that forever last breath?

I recently watched a clip shared by the BBC about a 96-year-old lady who radiated kindness and calmness. Every day she walks her neighbours' dogs – neighbours unable to walk their much-loved pets due to illness. As if that wasn't enough giving, she then heads to a local rescue that she considers home and the dogs there, her family. And she walks them. Everyday this purpose makes her happy; it helps her live purposefully.

I hope I get to my nineties – for all the animals I'm meant to cross my path with and if I don't make it to that good age, I hope – really hope, there will be many to fill my shoes and the shoes of every rescuer who have made a difference – real life differences to animals starving, injured, or being abused. You see they will always be waiting for someone to come. They never give up on us; we shouldn't give up on them.

And back to my shoes – maybe one day shoes like mine will be the ones everyone aspires to walk in – not all the time! No, just some of the time. That would be enough. I'm learning to put on my other shoes again. Afterall wearing the same pair all the time means they'll quickly get worn out! Sometimes a change is indeed as good as a rest. But my feet will always be more at home in my wellies and in fields where rescue dreams unfold.

Mirror, Mirror, on the wall,
Who is the craziest of us all?

October, 21st, 2019

'Jaysus, are you one of those?' he laughed.

'One of what?' I asked, purposely. I knew what he meant as he looked into my front window as we chatted outside.

'Crazy Cat Ladies!' he answered. 'Thought you'd have more sense,' he added.

And that is where my politeness usually leaves the conversation and my 'no mercy' response takes over when these types of interactions come along. 'Burnt' comes to mind when it comes to the same 'ding dong' opinion.

'They are not mine, you know!'

'Who owns them?' He was curious now.

I decided to not answer him straight away but threw out a question instead. 'Do all your friends and family neuter their cats?'

'I wouldn't know. We had a cat at home!'

'Oh, OK, so she or he was neutered?'

'God, no,' he replied.

'I see.'

'How many do you have?'

'Too many!' I began to 'pretend count' with my fingers.

I then pointed out some of the cats and their back stories. How some were dumped cats and kittens. How some were abused and too nervous to rehome, and how some were feral because they were born to an unneutered feral mother and were impossible to handle. 'I never wanted any of them, you know! But nobody else would take them or rescues were too full to burden any further.'

I think he began to see my situation a little differently. But maybe it was wishful thinking on my part. It is draining to explain again and again to people who ask, why have I so many cats? Yes, sometimes I'm angry about my situation and sometimes I'm even embarrassed by the number I have. But with me they are fed, sheltered and cared for. The main thing is: not one of them will be responsible for bringing one more kitten into this world.

'Right,' he nearly whispered. His laugh was gone – especially after I told him the weekly food bill and the combined veterinary costs.

Feeling a little bad for his initial joke falling – not flat, but into a cauldron of fire, I said I would lighten the mood. 'Sure, you could become the first Crazy Cat Man! I can give you your starter pack!'

'No thanks,' he quickly replied. 'Never liked cats myself!'

Well that answer got him a furry kitten into his hands and after a few minutes she was purring, and he was mesmerised.

I told him how Autumn was found in an abandoned building by a lady walking her dogs. She couldn't keep one kitten, so she handed her into the local vets. They called me as they couldn't keep her either.

I guess the moral of the story is: when you see someone with a lot of cats, ask yourself: how many were abused and dumped? How many are unwanted family pets? But there will be one uniform fact: they all came from unneutered mommy cats. Then ask yourself, do you really think that 'crazy cat lady' wants so many cats? And then you might ask yourself, 'how can I help?'

I am neither crazy or was ever really crazy about cats, but I don't like suffering and the cats I have – well the cats in my life are the easiest guests I have ever had. There is always room for one cat in everybody's home. Help lessen the burden of the CCLs. And if you have a cat, for crazy cat ladies' sakes – GET HER or HIM NEUTERED! If you don't – well it's you that's the crazy one! Along with cruel, selfish, inconsiderate…… I could go on!

Before I go from this post, I want to acknowledge all the cats who suffer terribly at the hands of humans. Prince who came to this house ten years ago. He came with some of the worst burns. His back was an open wound. Prince endured weekly essential cleansing of his wound that over time looked like it would never close. This affectionate cat has crossed paths with humans who decided one way to move him on was to throw boiling water on him. He has now moved on from them – thanks to a vet who took a chance on bringing the wound together. Despite unimaginable pain, this handsome ginger cat constantly reaches out his paw for love. Can you imagine his fate only for being rescued?

I guess if caring enough or too much about cats is crazy – well, I'll gladly wear that badge!

More than just politics

October 31st, 2019

Newstalk Breakfast gave airtime to a member of the new Animal Welfare Political party during the week. There is something a bit 'untuned' about this station when it comes to any topic related to animals. One of the presenters the other morning had an issue with the word 'sentient' in relation to animals. He questioned it in a 'jokey way'! How can someone who juggles all sorts of political and sensitive news stories on a day-to-day basis struggle with animals being sentient? Last time I checked we don't unplug them or take out batteries! Is it too much for some people to accept that animals feel an array of emotions – in fact sometimes even more than we do? Is it to get some people off the hook when it comes to addressing animal cruelty? If they don't feel – 'sure it's grand!' A lunch-time presenter from the same station one day dealt with the topic of vegetarianism with a stomach churning sneery attitude, and her lack of ability to just accept people's reasons for not eating meat was later reinforced when she later talked to a meat eater and made veiled jokes about veganism.

Anyway, back to politics! This country needs an animal welfare party – for all the obvious reasons but if you really think about it – the ill treatment and abuse of animals in this country is a reflection of our ills in general. And society's ills lead to more people in need of state's supports and interventions. I don't exaggerate! When I counsel young people, I am more concerned for the young people who have no empathy for animals, whilst in contrast, I have a sense of 'all will be OK' for the teenagers who take their dog for a walk or who volunteer at a rescue. Because when we can think of others outside of ourselves and support them – we have more a chance of managing our own stuff; we have less 'me me' thinking all the time and a higher level of emotional intelligence. Less likely to become narcissistic and we all know the damage narcissists can do. Think Trump Terror!

I'm off the topic! I think those outside of the animal loving circle really need to explore why they are so resistant to looking at all animals as sentient beings.

Last night I took in another kitten – all alone in the world. She had found pallets in an unused building site and made that her safe spot. My neighbour heard her cries and took her from behind the stacked old pallets. He knew something was wrong and asked me to collect her. She is this tiny bundle of black fur and she was saturated with urine and starving as she stopped herself walking - such was her pain. Last night I sat up with her by the fire as I felt it was her last night in this world after the vet explained possible complications. I listened to her purring and watched her attempts to groom herself. Puppy pads and talcum powder have her in a constant dry bed as she can't move to the litter tray so just pees as she lies down. The second vet visit today has given her till Monday to see will prescribed meds work. If they don't – her time in this world will end Monday. But until then each day we will fight with her as she is a sentient being who enjoys being petted, loves her kitten milk, and craves to engage with the other rescues here. We love her!

Someone somewhere did not neuter her mum. And somewhere out there are her siblings. Just like the three tiny kittens caught in an Aldi car park during the week! No bigger than your hand and yet facing the world on their own because someone somewhere did not neuter their mum. And now they are another three sentient beings being cared for by the amazing An Cat Dubh.

So, why do we need a 'one trick pony' political party? Because animal welfare is in crisis in this country – not because we don't have the relevant legislation – Oh No! We have some of the best – ON PAPER! The problem is – it is NOT being ENFORCED by those paid to enforce it. Yes, we are going to need more than one trick to get named authorities in animal welfare legislation to do their job! But with a party there is more hope.

There is a foal on the motorway who will probably die this Winter. Her owners give her stale bread once a week and I give her hay when I can. They stole the bucket I left for water. She has been reported to the Department, but nobody ever followed up if she was taken! So yes, it would be great to have a party who will shine a spotlight on the horrific cruelty that exists in Ireland – whether it's the puppy farmers with their tomb like breeding facilities, whether it's a horse owner who thinks it's their right to own a horse to tether them at the side of a road, whether it's the greyhound industry that dumps greys like household rubbish, or Joe Soap who keeps a dog in his garden or on a chain with no interaction or shelter and minimum food! This party may be just about animals – but it's one of the biggest issues that this country needs to sort out. After all the Dalai Lama said, 'the health of a nation can be judged by how it treats its animals.' And we aren't too healthy at the moment!

Where a horse has no name:
Ireland's chronic equine crisis

November, 25th, 2019

In Ireland we have animal welfare legislation to be somewhat proud of, but as the saying goes, sadly 'it isn't worth the paper it's printed on'. Like Monopoly money – it covers the department on the board table, but it is worthless in the 'real world'! We are good at these things in Ireland: pretending we are really good at stuff – like loving animals like our own family. Now where have I heard that before? Oh, yes, as I held a miniature pony eating ragwort to survive whose bottom lip had been bitten off by the owner's dogs. Reported: twenty-five times to the department by a rescue centre, by me, and by concerned members of the public. 25 reports versus 0 visits by the (paid) authorities to act. If I told you what it took to get a vet out that I paid for – you would probably stop reading this! But the owner did say, he loved that tiny little defenceless pony, like his own family.

So, let's get the law into the spotlight! In case any (paid) nominated authority named in the animal welfare legislation has forgotten. 'If you own or keep a horse or similar animal, it must be microchipped and he/she must have an official identification document, known as a horse passport. These requirements are under EU Regulation 504/2008 which, along with later amendments, has been transposed into Irish law. They apply to all members of the horse family, including ponies, donkeys and crosses, officially known as equine animals.' In addition, 'if you keep the horse in a control area designated under the Control of Horses Act 1996, you must have a horse licence for it as well as the microchip and passport. You are liable for any injury or damage caused by your horse to other people or to property.'

Now could the legislation be any clearer? You could say as clear as when a traffic light goes red, you don't press on the brakes and speed through a pedestrian green light – because – well, you would be breaking the law and you might kill someone. Just like the thirty sulkies recently on the Cahir to Cashel road or the run-away cart and horse in Dublin City the other day. Yes, all owners breaking the law, and someone might have died as a result.

Yesterday My Lovely Horse Rescue (unpaid) went to the aid of a mare who had nearly buried herself in mud. She had an horrific leg injury and was down for hours. They did their best but the kindest thing for this poor mare was to put her to sleep. Of course, it would be a lovely thing to let the owner know – except this horse had not the required legal identity. No microchip. No owner has come forward either! Funny he hasn't checked on his mare in 24 hours or notified the guards that she is missing.

Tonight, MLHR are with Dublin Fire Brigade tending to another mare down with her foal. Now if the owner was responsible or identifiable, Dublin Fire Brigade would not be there and the volunteers at MLHR would be mucking out stables, doing the night feeds, or God forbid, at home relaxing.

Today I fed a stallion at the side of the motorway. He stands on gravel. Thousands of people drive by him every day. For most he is of little significance. The truth is – the land here is starved of anything for him to forage on. It is NRA land so it's not a green pasture, but I'm now keeping him alive with daily hay drops. If he would die over-night, I would stop feeding him immediately to get him away from his owner, but death by starvation is horrific. And more so for horses. Their stomach constantly produces acid. So, can you imagine what an empty stomach goes through? His owner has a lot of horses and does not own one blade of grass. Reported to the authorities; he still has a lot of horses. In one year alone, twenty-five of his horses died.

In nine years, I have never seen any appropriate or proactive intervention from department vets or officials when I have reported starving or dying horses. A rescue friend in another county says she gets support from her department veterinary officer. But shouldn't the law be the law and not be dependent on the personality of the official. One pony I dealt with was locked in a shed for twelve days with no food or water. The department veterinary officers visited the owners and had a 'chat'. A local man broke the lock on the shed and I had to buy the pony to keep him alive. No, not the answer but a law that keeps giving nothingness makes ordinary decent people either into criminals or

144

colluders by feeding these people's animals or buying them to save them. I did get a letter from the department telling me I was part of the problem. Now that's ironic! If I'm part of the problem – what would they be?

Did I mention the barrister in the West who kept a thoroughbred mare and foal by the coast during the harshest of Winters with no shelter and with bare pickings? His horses were seized only to be returned to him by a judge. You could say the law is an ass but that would belittle all the equines right now licking moss, eating mud, or drinking from dirty puddles to stay alive. That would belittle all the foals being backed or hitched up to sulkies. That would minimise the pain of thoroughbreds left uncovered and starving this Winter by 'should never have horses' owners.

To get emotive now is not what the illegally held horses of Ireland need or the legally held abused ones. They need our Minister to get out of his 'meat meetings' and get down to equine rescues and listen to them. They are not clocking off for the weekends or after 6; they are not the ones reading cruelty cases on a database and dismissing them. They are the ones out there on the ground being proactive. If you took them out of the equation – imagine – actually, I don't want to, and you probably don't want to either.

I often ask the owners of horses I keep an eye on – 'tell me, what are their names?' And they never have any! No chip, no passport, no land, and no name. But there is one definite in this

145

argument: the law is on the side of these horses. It says so in black and white!

Do you ever think about all the car accidents involving a horse being on the road? Did you ever think that might be a horse breaking out to get to grass? If you were starving and in pain – wouldn't you do anything to stay alive? So, enforcing the law matters to them mostly and to us! My life or your life might just depend on it.

Last night the mare put to sleep to end her suffering was named as Francesca. Remember that name. Remember the hours she spent waiting in cold mud seeping into her severed leg! Remember she should not have been there if the legislation to protect her was enforced or acted as a real deterrent to these cruel cowboy owners. Imagine what she went through for hours in horrific pain all by herself. Imagine . . .

Naughty or Nice

December 7th, 2019

If there was a naughty or nice list (for adults!), the nice list would feature a lot of names from the rescue world we have become accustomed to. In some of their cases there should probably be a 'too nice for their own good!' list too. You see, some really are; others have healthy boundaries ensuring they stay 'just nice', and some actually verge between the naughty and the nice list. But that's for another day!

I know many rescuers who would like to go back to just volunteering whenever suits or fostering the odd cat, dog or pony. Some would like to just go back to their lives as planned with their own animals and spend spare time with loved ones. Some would like to take a shower without having numerous curious kittens looking on and some would like to look in their shopping basket and see a few items for themselves and not have to explain to the person on the till that 'no, I don't have a fetish for sardines!' But they don't and they can't. Their selflessness outweighs the need to retrieve their old lives back. Lives on pause for now or forever. Because Ireland has an animal welfare crisis and the only people on the frontline are mainly rescuers.

The lack of basic humanity has thrown some rescuers 'to the lions!' A simple example is the unneutered family cat – well, that results in a lot of kittens born because one cat wasn't neutered! Someone has to intervene. Of course, it's easier to neuter one cat compared to all the ones that will be born as a result of ordinary Joe 'I don't care' Soap. And what about all the dogs in the pound that rescues have to make room for every week. Most of these are surrenders and strays. Probably coming from the same context: someone, somewhere, didn't care enough for them to not give up on them. And then, what about our chronic equine crisis. When owners won't feed them, it is left to someone else to or rescue them, in the absence of enforced animal welfare legislation. So yes, it would be nice for rescuers to just be plain old naughty sometimes but with Joe 'I couldn't give a hoot' Soap, and a Minister for Agriculture who appears either oblivious or apathetic, they are going nowhere from that list.

We can always hope that in 2020 so much of this hard, soul destroying, heart-breaking but rewarding work won't be left up to the same usual suspects.

.

You're a disgrace!

I always wanted to be liked. But that changed the day I saw a pony tethered to a fence at the side of a road covered in mud. I didn't know it changed: necessity changed it. You see, the minute I saw her, I was shifted from my semi-selfish world to a selfless one. Again, it was not by choice: necessity moved me.

Before I knew it, I was buying hay, before I knew it, I was climbing many diverse obstacles for this pony. Before I knew it, one bale a day became seven, sometimes ten. Before I knew it, I stopped feeling the pain of a bad back (an injury I got when I was wearing 4-inch-heels on my way to interview a DJ for a magazine! I slipped on tiles and fell badly.) Yes, before I realised it, I was feeding sometimes 10 to 25 hungry horses a day. One day I fed 100, in fields, along motorways and tied in sites – before a curfew landed due to extreme weather.

Yes, before I knew it, I was gathering a fan base of people who gave out about me. People who believed traveller horses should starve to death and people who thought rich farmers would never 'not feed' their animals. People said they wouldn't feed them once I was: when the reality is, there is a type of owner who doesn't care if they are fed or not. Some people believed that if you rang this magic number, the department's veterinary officers or other officials would descend and sprinkle fairy dust to magically fix Ireland's chronic equine crisis. Horses are dying of hunger and in the majority of cases, nobody with the authority to do something comes to the rescue.

One day along came a spider…. yes, like one of those venomous ones. She pulled up – probably on her way to mass and told me I was a 'disgrace' for feeding 'traveller horses'. I pointed up to a farm and told her I'm feeding three donkeys there that the farmer is not feeding. She ignored that point, because she knew him, and went on to tell me I should be ashamed of myself. I held a bale as she spoke, I never let go, despite the twine cutting into my hands. There was a horse over my shoulder waiting for that hay to sprinkle her patch of ground that was hard after severe frost.

I never gave her my reasons that day, because I was tired of always explaining my reasons for feeding hungry horses: my reasons for nearly giving up everything I ever had – both monetary and personally to keep horses both alive and free of suffering. I did it because I believed if I could keep them alive – one day I or somebody else would get them out. If they couldn't be seized, if they were let down by authorities, I would find more money to buy them (I know – part of the problem!).

The mare looking over the gate and over my shoulder was a beautiful majestic girl. I fed her from a bucket at a few months old when she was ripped from her mother way too young. I loved her from the moment her shiny baby head tried to reach over the council steel gate to feel some comfort.

And the years passed, I watched her grow, always promising her – one day you will know green fields and care. A promise I made to many. She was moved with the others from field to field, from bits of ground to other bits of ground. And yes, I followed them with hay – day after day. And then came her day. I couldn't believe it. Finally, it was over. The plan had worked: to keep her alive till her rescue day came.

Today I tried to drive but I had to pull in. I couldn't see through my tears. Today I heard she died. And before I knew it, my heart broke another bit, for another beautiful brave horse that had tried to survive against all odds. I do believe horses maintain hope within them for a better life when the life they lead is one of trying to survive. I often think of a very emotional rescue in Laois, when the rescuer was only allowed to take two mares out. They were completely emaciated and in foal. What stays with me is how all the others in the barren field lined up to go to. A proud stallion with a body condition that bore all the hallmarks of years of starving, never been wormed and probably on a sulky from a young age. I often think 'did he make it?' Sometimes I hope he didn't. Death is often a welcome for these horses when rescue is not possible. How very sad is that? I as someone who loves animals so much, I often pray they will die quickly to get away from their owners. Death is a blessing in disguise.

Another rescuer told me today that sometimes animals

who are treated badly, when they get to a safe place, they can give up. Because they know they do not have to put up a fight anymore and because they are in a place of care to leave this world. I told another rescuer, that she had died, and he told me to remember the ones we do get to save and do get to go on to have a life. And that is how some rescuers keep going through the constant loss and heartache.

But today was about her. Remembering her. And realising I'm not a disgrace after all. I can't do what I used to do for all these horses around me that are still starving and struggling. There is no money left – a bit extra to feed 2 or 3 in bad places. But worse again, I'm beginning to lose my courage and I'm not sure why? I have this raging voice within that wants to scream for justice for her and to make the owner realise what his cruel choices did to her. I decided today I was going to tell him what he did to her: his terrible treatment a few months before her day to get out, sealed her fate. Someone stopped me. He reminded me that 'he doesn't care.' You see, they don't. They really don't. Yet they want horses that they don't have to care about. Those that starve horses may not care but those paid to care need to do more. Remember this story when you go to vote. Horses are suffering unimaginable pain because the law is not being enforced. They are another type of disgrace: they that leave this endless and difficult work for rescuers to do.

We are a developed country. This chronic cruelty crisis should not exist in a developed society. It is unacceptable that it is blatantly allowed. No, it may not be a voting issue for some but it should be a voting issue for those of you tired of animals suffering out there.

Remember that word 'disgrace' next time someone asks you for their vote. Remember this foal that grew up to die at four.

Rock-a-bye-baby

July 26th, 2020

I was half asleep last night when an empty horse box left our yard.
I was awake when it returned at 3am. A big box with a tiny foal a
few weeks old inside. Yes, another one. Foal season is up there
now with kitten season in the rescue world as one you dread. You
see most arrive in ill-health, and at a few weeks old, well, milk
replacer does not come close to warm, motherly milk. Their cries
for their mommy cut deeply into a heart that has many breaks for
them – breaks left by all the others that came before.

    Let me tell you about Cillian. He was thrown onto the
streets of Limerick City. God forbid, the owners let a foal stay
with his mum. I mean he's a boy after all and he doesn't have that
perfect, coloured coat. Yes, let's start again boys and get that mare
(his mum) covered again with that big piebald who has covered
half of Limerick city. Never mind the STIs. Never mind the
suffering of a mare who year after year is put into foal and tries to
keep herself alive to keep her unborn foal sustained inside. A mare
I fed for years had enough of being constantly put into foal, so she
resisted the stallion and tried to fight to keep him off her. Her
owners wanted to help her – help her stand still. So, they tied her

back legs with blue rope. They left marks that were slow to fade. All I could do was love her more and make sure she had adequate nutrition to keep her well and her foal within.

Before Cillian arrived last weekend there was a foal called Oran, born to a thoroughbred mare. Yes, someone sold their in-foal thoroughbred mares to a man who dumps foals devoid of that much sought-after colour scheme. The thoroughbred mares probably came from yards with buckets of fresh water and grassy paddocks. Now they are tied to poles – adding to the equine dots in a busy urban landscape. Luckily for Oran, great rescue friends took him in. But the man who bought his mother needed him gone ASAP so she could be put into foal with his coloured stallion. Who are you that sells your 'looked-after' horse to mean streets and meaner people?

Why should you care? Well, I guess none of us should be OK with cruelty and we all should seek a society where laws are enforced. All these horses are illegally held: the ones running in estates, at the side of motorways, and tied to fences. The ones with wormy bellies, bones protruding, and that look of loss in their eyes.

If the law was enforced, they would never be there, and Cillian might just be waking up this morning suckling off his mum. Instead he's in another box on the way for emergency veterinary treatment. You see, this morning I tried to get him to drink from a bottle. This morning I saw a baby who just didn't want to be in this world anymore. He wanted to give up, so we

155

have to do the opposite and be his lifeline till he wants to live again. That is if the last few days of starvation haven't decided his fate already.

The new Minister of Agriculture better steer the welfare ship better than the last minister. And he better tell his well-paid welfare crew that it's time to do their bloody job or get off board.

When the only choice is to run

August 7th, 2020

I have two tricky rescue dogs. Tricky meaning, I have to keep a close eye on them. Paudie was found dodging Galway City traffic which tests even those of us in cars. Imagine being a tiny JR on a busy Halloween night in the middle of the city's busiest junctions. Yes, he stood out. My sister managed to follow him into an industrial estate. When a lone dog crosses your path, there is always that hopeful voice within that maybe he has an owner missing him. Then you look again for all the tell-tale signs of lack of human input or cruel input. Yes, little Paudie who was about 8 when rescued had a lamb ring around his tail. His owner decided he would prefer his older dog to have a docked tail. His owner nearly killed him. Paudie ended up spending days at the vets. His tail was badly infected. He was a lucky boy to have been found in time and not so lucky to have an owner who takes surgical procedures into his own selfish, cruel hands.

So, back to tricky! Paudie and Sasha have to be walked in areas with no people or other dogs. So that means finding remote areas where they can have a run off-lead. Yes, the things we do for those we love. They would never bite another dog, but they tend to get fearful and defensive – 'bark worse than bite' scenario. They bark non-stop to let others know 'no one is going to hurt me again!' So, most of our morning walks are taken in a swamp-like area under a bridge that is part of a new road network. So, the other morning our remote area was the usual 'wildlife silent'. Just me, the dogs but one other person.

The morning before I was driving another set of 'not tricky' rescues to their forest walk where they meet lots of other dogs. On the way there, an older lady caught my eye: she was old-school beautiful. No make-up – just sparkle: the inside-out type that is innate. She smiled as she crossed the road. I decided she had just stepped out of some glamorous 'camera-lights-action' scenario.

So, how did this lady end up 24 hours later in 'our swamp'. We were the Shreks and she was the fairy-like Godmother that magically appeared.

It's funny how sometimes when we are met with difficult or strange scenarios, we walk a bit quicker as our mind tries to do quick processing – deciding is this a flight or fight scenario? Or maybe just blocking out something we can't process.

She waved and I waved back, and I went ahead with our walk. When the walk was finished, we passed again, and I quickly took a closer look as she sat under the bridge at 8am in the morning. I took in her bags and I heard an apology. She was sorry for being there. My trickies didn't even bark.

So, I got into my car, drove towards the end of the road

that brings me onto a roundabout and home. Except I never made it to the roundabout. I turned around and drove back. She was walking in the direction out also. I stopped, got out, and automatically told the dogs not to bark as I usually do when I stop to talk to anyone. They still didn't. The conversation started with, 'Are you OK?' followed by 'Did you sleep there last night?' She answered 'Yes' to both questions. But added 'it was so cold last night!' When concrete is your bed, you are robbed of any warming comforts.

I took in her beautiful, tailored coat that was showing the signs of a life on concrete. But her hair was perfect, and she had that big, wide Hollywood smile. Did she want help? 'No' was her definite decision. I asked for a minute to check the car for anything I had. There was just 6 euros for her to get a coffee. She didn't want to take it. The dogs still didn't bark. She didn't have a phone, but I made her take my phone number. We parted ways. I live close-by, so I said goodbye but was secretly hoping to get to my house and back to her with a little bit more to help pay for accommodation. And so, I did. I met her again walking back towards town. I indicated and pulled in and let down the window, and as I held up traffic, I handed her some money. One of my tricky dogs was nearly out the passenger window as he put his paws up on the open window and took in this lovely lady again. There was still no barking. They had a moment. She looked at him and he at her and she said, 'he's so kind looking'. I imagine he felt the exact same given his reaction. It was hard for her to accept the help. There was a promise she would ring me later from a borrowed phone.

Where is this post going? I'm not quite sure. I do hope she's OK and one day she doesn't have to keep running. I did ring services in case she did ring. I wanted to have all the information she might need. Some people want to desperately run so far away from their own worlds where difficult emotional memories and certain people they fear exist. And, yes, sometimes the only option is to run. Just like all the dogs people report who can't be caught when they approach them. They associate people with terrible experiences and memories.

A week ago, I made a promise, that I would never regret again not getting something right when it comes to an animal or person in need. This promise was made because of a young collie locked into a horse box for two years. Living in his own waste and being provided with a pint of milk a day. I heard about this dog a year ago. When I did, I reported him to a rescue as I knew they had better contacts than me. I then packed my car with food, a big bed and bowls. I had to try do something until there was an official intervention; I wanted to make life a bit better for him. The owner met me and quickly turned his back on me and told me to take my stuff back. In the background was an old horsebox in the middle of a grassy field with faint sounds of a dog. Yes, it's very difficult when you're there, so close to a dog in need, yet focusing on getting around a very stubborn owner to accept help. So, I went back to the rescue and told them he refused help and suggested we could put up a dog run – an option if he couldn't be seized. You see, like many, I've heard the hard to comprehend excuse 'but they have food and shelter' many times when it came to reporting dogs locked away from the world or in chains. Food and shelter deemed enough to sustain a sentient being. I was thinking this would also be the excuse that would keep him in a box forever. So, I always think of alphabetic alternative plans. They often go past B.

To cut a long story short, that was a year ago. I don't know what happened me, but this collie went out of my mind. I was told he would be seized if conditions didn't improve, but I even forgot that until I reread messages recently. You see I heard he was still there a year later last week. Straight away I began contacting the Guards and the Department's welfare section. But to really cut a long story short, it was another rescuer who used the medium of social media as armour to fight for this dog. It worked. He was seized and the last time I saw him, he was on a couch with a waggy tail and a caring hand on his head.

So, after Barney the collie, I decided to keep following up on concerns until I know the problem is resolved whether for an animal or a human. And that is why last Tuesday, I turned my car around to talk to that lady. I didn't want to have any regrets.

Yes, there was something special about her. My one eyed Paudie's little paw on her trusting hand on an open window told me so. But, like some dogs, some people also have been hurt too much to ever trust humans again. So, they just keep running… not to stand still for anyone.

When a rescue unpacks:
the emotionally difficult work behind the photos

August 31ˢᵗ, 2020

'Courage is fear holding on a minute longer.'

G.S.Patton

Some of you are probably familiar with the counselling term 'unpacking' and all of us are probably over-familiar with the term 'emotional baggage' – whether our own or someone else's. Many therapists would say, until we unpack, piece by piece, all that 'hard to face' emotion stuffed in randomly – well, we will never get to simply BE – be who we are really meant to be or have space for more positive emotions. Makes sense? Imagine living your daily life weighed down by a heavy bulging, burdensome suitcase. Yep, we get triggered, we get moody, and we simply get worn out. And too often those who care most, get to feel cared about the least. Animals are no different and being non-verbal, can you imagine feeling all these emotions without having the words to make sense of them? So, too often, certain emotions present as challenging behaviours – just as ours does, when we don't use our words! Everything is to blame except what's in that 'suitcase'! It

162

is easier to point fingers of blame than look at what is really going on. It is a question we all could ask ourselves more.

Back to animals, before I realised my love for animals, sometimes I would hear or read about a dog PTS in a pound because of his temperament. Years later, I think of these vast number of dogs who never made it/or will make it to a rescue who would have worked on unpacking that emotional, canine baggage. Anger is a secondary emotion after all. It comes after a primary one – usually like fear, sadness, rejection, and yes, even feeling hungry or possessive over the sight of food.

When we adopt a dog, we usually open our hearts and homes to a dog 'ready to begin again' because their rescue or rescuer has done the time-consuming task of unpacking their emotional baggage. They try connect the triggers to the contents. They try join the dots to build a picture of needs and remedies, replace bad memories with good, break old habits and replace with new, and finally, try to create that secondary picture: what their new home should look like. Imagine taking on this task with many dogs, every day. Yes, just imagine!

And so that brings me to the 67th and 68th heartbeat that's fills another piece of my own heart: Tyke and Brie – Madra rescues – now well known as two of the Croga (courageous) Collies. They arrived on Friday morning with Madra's Carrie, who happened to give me grinds in dog behaviour supports specifically for Tyke and Brie. Of course, being an eager student, I hooked on to one technique I got quickly 'treat and retreat' until she politely pointed out that it might not work too well with Tyke! Well, he is blind after all!!! Oops!

Being locked away from the world amongst many others in a confined space is going to quickly fill that emotional case. Rescuing this family of collies from the only home they knew was just one part of a long process for Madra. From that day on, I can only imagine that the Croga Collies consumed their days and for some I'm sure many a sleepless moment. They had to figure out how each one could live in homes as pets.

It's like when the road divides or the luck of the draw. Can you imagine if they went to some pounds in this country? They would have lived and died with all that negative emotion/ experiences – never knowing any other life. Never knowing what it's like to just BE: be a carefree dog – be truly loved and cared for. How hard is it to just let dogs be?

When it comes to dogs hidden from the world or on chains, it is something that haunts me: dogs who live and die with a chain around their neck, or dogs who live and die in darkness. It is hard to believe that chaining a dog is legal in Ireland despite the 5 freedoms our animal welfare legislation is based on.

And so, on Friday two beautiful, soulful collies were lifted from Carrie's car, their crates were opened, and for the next few hours, time was given to ease them into their new surroundings. Unsure at first, but little tails didn't go between legs or heads didn't try to hide. They were ready to adapt and ready to explore. Because their rescuers took the time to unpack with them. We, as the people adopting, get to see them just be who they are now: Tyke, the handsome explorer and snoozer. Brie, bouncy and beautiful, who crawls over to you on her belly until she knows it's OK to play. Yes, their years of confinement has conditioned them and yes, scarred them, but they are scars that are part of who they are, they no longer define them fully. You see, like counselling, they got to be in a safe space with kind, knowledgeable people who walked the recovery road with them. And with no words, or no stories, their rescuers were not privileged to be able to just listen. They had to observe and observe and then show these very frightened dogs that it's OK to be afraid or even angry but 'here, this will make you feel less afraid!' That could be a cosy bed, a comforting toy, a walk with no other dogs or maybe with a dog, a walk on lead or maybe off-lead. Or simply just to sit with them.

On Saturday morning about 5:30am Brie was barking so I went out to her as she hadn't barked since she arrived. And at that moment through sleepy eyes, I sat on a slow feeder (to avoid the dewy ground) and just simply said,' it's going to be OK, Brie,' and after a few minutes she went back into her bed and fell fast asleep.

Over the last few days, I've caught Brie and Tyke having these special, short but sweet moments of togetherness. Brie licks him and he licks her back and she bounces around him. Of course, I'd like to think if they had words, they would say, 'Can you believe it? Can you just believe it? We made it to a place called home! Life is truly amazing!'

Functioning with a broken heart

September 6th, 2020

The above poignant headline is borrowed from Mundy. Yesterday I listened to Jarlath Regan's interview with the Offaly artist. I'm a late starter to podcasts and it was my brother who opened up my 'under-used' iPhone features to me. When you are busy out on a yard or doing long distances – podcasts are now my 'go-to' for company and to get that intellectual fix.

And back to Mundy and that line that resonated with me. To put it into context, he was discussing his sudden arrival into a world of tour dates, media interviews, and one hotel room after the other. He really was open and honest when he shared an insight into literally 'keeping the show on the road' whilst dealing with a broken heart – whether it comes from a family illness or a grief that permeates your mindscape whilst maintaining that celebrity sparkle people expect. He never divulged what was the cause of his. But he gave the listeners an insight into the human behind the mic and burst what we often imagine as a glamorous, care-free, celebrity bubble. Two diverse worlds can live parallel to each other and ironically in a type of harmony. Sure, most of us can relate to that, just on a less public, life stage.

And what has that got to do with rescuing and animal advocacy. I guess his interview reminded me of two things: my after school days sometimes spent sitting beside him in my father's car, as I waited for him to finish work to get a lift home, and my life full of dreams and expectations that had nothing ever to do with animals. Whilst I listened to his interview, I fished my long-term memory for my seventeen-year-old self's shared conversations, and who I showed to the world. Memory can be the biggest let-down at times. The more you try to remember, the less you seem to remember at that given time. I don't think I shared this dream with any of my friends, but I did have this thing about being famous: that it would sort out all my life's woes! How very innocent of me. I grew up being told as a young child how Princess Grace of Monaco was a distant relation, so I watched her movies with a real interest and much admiration. I guess she became a type of role-model, and I attempted to carve out a career in television and radio. Radio became a passion of mine, and for a while I balanced it well with teaching and counselling.

When you rescue, have rescues, advocate for animals – you really do a superb job at functioning. The truth be told: the majority of us just become really good at functioning. Our hearts ache: our hearts have broken many times, for the animals we rescue and who are completely broken, the animals we lost, and the ones we never 'got out' before it was too late. Yet, we function. We put on that 'keeping the show on the road' face – without the adoration of fans, the plush hotel rooms, and the pay cheque. Yes, we function. One foot in front of the other, one day at a time, and one rescue at a time, we function.

A broken heart never fully mends: there is no miracle cast. But it can be soothed. It can function and function well. It's important to remember that: a broken heart needs to be minded whilst 'keeping your show on the road'. I have to say that some of my happiest and purest moments have being a frightened foal coming to me after being thrown from a van, or an extremely nervous dog licking my hand. My memory tends to remember these moments. And that makes sense, as we tend to remember what impacts us the most emotionally.

Today on my birthday I wish I could for one day gather the heroic broken-hearted rescuers I know and launch them onto a big stage with their names in lights. Yes, they should be celebrated more. There are many types of heroes out there, but today I want to remember the ones who wear my kind of 'heart on their sleeves'. More of these people should be household names because it's what the world needs more of, I feel. To celebrate those who continually give to others, who change lives and who create lights in bleak tunnels. Animal rescuers don't just rescue animals, but the very animals they rescue often bring families together or complete families – even create a family for a person on their own.

Some of the most inspiring, resilient, funny, and entertaining people I know happen to work in rescue or are part of 'that world' in some shape or form. Their stories can draw tears, smiles and laughter all at once. Now, who else could do that?

No place like home

September 26th, 2020

We all can have different reactions to the word home. For some regardless of the negative connotations – home is still home: it's all you know and you long for it. For those of us lucky enough, home is safety; home is love.

When I first started working in secondary school settings, I was always struck by some young people who literally lived in houses of horrors and who despite getting into foster care and away from very broken homes, still wanted to go home. One boy kept running away from foster care and would often be found sleeping or sitting on the doorstep of a house (his home) where no one was ever home. It was home to him: it was all he knew. The tragedy is some will never know any other normal and the cycle continues. A probably greater tragedy and wrong (if it's possible to measure) is when someone has a safe and familiar home, and someone plucks them from it – which brings this post to the word normal and what we normalise.

I read an article yesterday about collies in Mayo where they live in unimaginable deplorable conditions. Some are kept in car boots. A rescuer said she is considered a troublemaker for highlighting it and some have bought dogs from here to simply save them. During the week a rescuer called me about an animal in an urban setting at risk. What both these owners have in common is a twisted, concerning mindset, when it comes to keeping animals – not to mention lack of empathy. However, I can vouch for this: not all people who hoard or who are cruel to animals 'have something wrong with them'. Some do it because they can and they get away with it. Some are just plain old evil and choose to be so, and it is not down to a mental health problem. Some people get a kick out of being cruel in the same way you get a kick out of being kind. I said to the rescuer on the phone: 'you are ringing me (no authority to intervene) to ring someone else (with equally no authority) to help you (no authority), to get the animal out!' and I went on to add 'aren't we meant to be able to call an authorised officer?' and that's where we both did a U-turn on that futile path of being actually able to call a person with the authority to act! That would be a normal thing to do but normal has yet to find the rescue world. Rescuers search for it, hope for it, but are actually the architects of it for a lot of animals they save. They find homes, and often create another space for another animal they have crossed paths with within their own home.

A Guard once said to me: 'there is something wrong with ye! A bit touched!' I looked at a woman in uniform who previously had normalised a kitten being kicked around a kitchen (the video was posted to social media). I looked at a Guard who normalised a tiny dog kept on a chain with a 'falling-apart' box for shelter. A Guard owned the dog. This is a woman who tried to convince me there was something wrong with me and 'my kind'. I don't think I have to argue who really has to fix their mindset and moral compass.

No, it's also not normal that our government has granted a renewed license for hares to be netted, ripped from their natural terrain, to be placed into a public arena where adults and children roar and scream at hounds to chase them, to fill them with fear, and to toss them in the air. What is not normal is that 77% of people said they did not want hare coursing anymore. Is that normal? To not listen to the majority. To not listen to the CEO of the ISPCA? What is the constant truth: it isn't normal to cruelly intervene in a natural habitat for man's entertainment and need fulfillment.

So, I write this on top of a hill with two brave collies by my side. Their home is a piece of my heart and a tiny piece of our yard where they have a place to call home. They don't ask for much but what they need is all they want: safety, care, love, food, and kindness. Owners who don't provide adequate care not only are breaking the law, but they miss out on a dog who wants to be by their side, a dog who wags his/her tail, a dog that wants to love them unconditionally. They are robbing them of a normal home. If you cannot care for your animals, allow someone else to.

A clinical definition of sadism is to derive pleasure from inflicting or witnessing pain/suffering. Our government has given the thumbs up to a 'sport' that nurtures and gives a license to an extremely barbaric and sadistic activity: a hare running for its life from hounds trained to kill the hare.

They say to teach empathy you have to put someone in someone else's shoes/paws. I wish I could place that collie owner in Mayo in a boot for one day and I wish I could put our TDs who voted for hare coursing into an arena where they are chased down by two animals trained to chase them and cause harm as we all cheered on. I do not jest: In most cases people have to feel the suffering they inflict to stop inflicting it themselves.

The photos you will never see

This week I was shown a photo of a stunning coloured mare side by side with a young woman. We all know the saying: a picture speaks a thousand words. But for many of us who have been through those testing 'befores' and rewarding 'afters' or those 'it's hard to believe' 'then and nows' – these photos put us back on the overly-rode emotional rollercoaster where no tickets apply: something innate in you pushes you back on over and over again as you recall and remember.

No, this isn't just any sweet photo of a horse with her adoring owner: it is that and more. The mare's eyes seem to look down the lens, and her thoughts maybe travel across countries and overseas back to her 'before' – one I shared with her. The mare in the photo is Erin, a beautiful coloured girl who I came across in a field covered in whip marks and one of her eyes unable to see. She is the mare I got into a box to get her out, only to have to let her go as she was kicking the box with such ferocity that she was about to come through it. I was in the box with her, seeing her absolute fear where she went to a place where I was no longer by her side. I was quickly taken out the jockey door and the ramp

174

came down. There was a plan to get a better box as we never imagined her reaction to being boxed. However, her owner decided he wanted to keep her. And I then had to accept, Erin would never know anything but here: a vast swamp.

However, after a road traffic accident, Erin and her friends in another field got seized and that is how Erin made it to her new forever home far away from here. Bella didn't make it – soon after her seizure, she had to be PTS, the damage done prior to seizure meant she would never recover. I can't tell you how much that hurt. I had rescued her mother previously and she only got six months in her rescue space. Years of probably eating ragwort before I found her had caused irreversible damage. I asked many vets to see her but every day she continued to fade away more. Her owners surrendered her, and she spent six months in the loving care of Forgotten Horses Ireland, where she experienced simple normality.

The craving to put my head to Erin's was overwhelming. I can't and probably never will again. You see it's hard to love an animal that will never be yours – I guess it's similar to loving someone who has given their heart to someone else. The emotion is similar. But Erin was never mine. I remember I was often shouted at from passing cars – 'feed your horse' or 'go get a job!' Or 'you're a disgrace feeding traveller horses'. Many presuming I was the owner or a rescuer with nothing better to do.

Back in the day, when I lived in Ennis, I would get up in the morning, travel to a hay yard, and fill my car with hay, hard feed and fill bottles of water. There were horses in desperate need of feed every day – they lived in swamps like Erin or along motorways. Their owners' belief: they can live off nothingness.

And so back to the photo. The photo that speaks a thousand words of heartbreak, of friends who rallied to help me pay for hay when I faced financial ruin as a result – hard to believe but my hay feeding programme, vet fees, farriers, transport, along with other related costs exceeded over 50,000 over 5 years. Always the objective was to keep them alive till their rescue day came. Yes, I did keep some of them alive, some did die in these terrible places, and some died just after being rescued. I know it's a part I still struggle with. But Erin is looking into the camera as if to say: 'I made it out and I'm home!'

I know grief – like many of you reading this – the feeling of death of a loved one cutting a slice of you away and stealing it forever. But what fills the cutting void in time is memories – memories of them that keeps your loved ones in your 'here and now'. Yes, I cry often for the animals I loved that were never mine – the ones who never got to get away. And that is my tribute to them: to remember their names and to share their names. So today I'm remembering Summer, Holly, and her daughter Bella.

We will always have the 'before and afters' and the 'then and nows' – many in our life-times. I guess we just have to make the most of the 'afters' and the happy 'nows' and strive to make the most of them – whilst remembering how we got there when we fall again.

But if you're reading this, when you can – help those who are constantly searching for and creating 'the happy ever afters' for those who can't do it for themselves. There are a lot of these people out there who could do with your support right now.

So, this is a photo of Erin, her owner will never see. There are so many horse owners out there who will never get to see the beautiful potential in their horses. They won't because they will neither feed them adequately nor make them feel safe enough to stand still beside them without being tied up. There is another foal I rescued who has now risen to be nearly 17 hands and has become a photo of equine perfection. And no, her owner will never see her photo either. They probably would not believe me if I told them: 'this was your horse!' Simply because, they will never recognise the difference care makes.

.

A crazy little thing called home

November 8th, 2020

Home seems to be a recurring theme these days in my posts, but I guess it's the nature of the business here. I'm going to make a somewhat informed guess and say that most of us have said at some stage or at many stages in our lives: I just want to go home. HOME! And for a suspended magical second – home is possible, home is perfect, and home will make everything right again. Most homes are and were far from perfect but it's our inner child within us who still wants to run home. It's House on the Prairie or Highway to Heaven; it's escaping reality and giving us that magical momentary feeling. Even in its most chaotic or broken – home is still home and for those of us lucky enough to have a constant loving home – home is an arm of love constantly reaching out, ready to catch us when we fall.

This week I moved some rescue cats into Hilltop Sanctuary, where I now reside. They were being taken from a live-in situation in a town house with a catio to a small farm busy with different animals. So, we decided to build them a home away from home here. Familiar beds and blankets were dotted here and there, along with their toys. From the minute they arrived, and the cat

178

boxes opened, there were cries for home; the diverse climbers and toys were ignored, and a collective grief was formed. I knew there would be an initial settling in period, but nothing prepared me for their sadness. Cats are very attached to their territory and I had removed them from their familiar one. This was not home. Being an empath can be a blessing and a curse: I was consumed with guilt which was reinforced by their baby-like pleas to bring them home. I felt all their sadness at once. It made me think of pets dumped in the dark of the night: how desperately upsetting and frightening it must be for them.

In the last few days, we lost one of our latest rescues. A 17- hand-mare who looked like she stepped out of a fairy-tale book. But her life was far from a fairy-tale – thanks to an owner who looks and talks like a knowledgeable horse owner, and would be respected in his circles – yet he left his horses out into fields logged with water for the Winter and never knew Ali was down for 3 days with an excruciating infection. I guess animals are truly dependant on their owner who writes their story dictated by their empathy or lack of. Her owner didn't spend long on her story. He was the villain and she was his money-maker, foal-maker. And as rescuers you are akin to an editor who can get lucky enough to rewrite a villainous script. You get to change the ending with the help of diverse characters all wanting the same: for a mare let down so badly to go to a caring home. Rescuers don't think about the costs of change or healing: there is a new narrative to work on, a life to be saved and a happy-ever-after to complete. Money will be found somewhere. And when you are busy planning and happy for her, the phone rings and the pen in your mind drops like a knife into your heart. The equine hospital can't save her, and they ring the sanctuary for permission to end her suffering – a man-made one. But what about the home waiting for her? What about what was meant to be? And so, you swing from sadness to anger in seconds and back again until you accept. You accept that Ali is home in another way. Home should be free of pain and suffering and she is there now. As hard as it is for us that cared deeply for her and washed and bandaged her wounds and helped her with her pain, our upset is eased by what could have been if we had not been told about her. We made her pain less; we cared for her as if she was our own, and we were part of her last journey to her final home. It never gets easy and the day it does is the day it has changed you.

So, what about us and our search (sometimes) for home when we are in one. What do we do when the one we crave for is no more or maybe never was? When you have animals in your life, you are really their home. Wherever you are, they are home. I guess we can try learn from this. Home is within us all. And if that is the case, it's important to make ourselves resilient, content, and work on that 'happy with ourselves' life module that we can ace or fail depending on us. The good thing is we can keep repeating the learning until we simply love ourselves and the lesson is over.

Yes, just like the cats who cry to go home – it's allowing

ourselves to acknowledge that upset and explore what it is about 'home' we crave that might actually be within us to create.

The Christmas Magnifying Glass
Oh, Yes, there is!

December, 2020

I'm privileged as a counsellor to be able to hear people's stories – usually in a completely raw state: no filter, no editing, or no 'putting on a face'. And because of my role I can remind clients that they are not alone in their pain, their grief, broken-heart-ness, loneliness or whatever troubles them. But the collective experience is no executioner of pain, however it does help to quieten the 'why me?' internal monologue that can drown out any other rational or kinder voice. Besides, it's often not a case of 'why me?' but 'this is the reason why'. There are of course tragic exceptions but usually it is the choices we make that plant the seeds to the answers of 'why me?' But making wrong choices is akin to putting on weight – it's damn easy but damn hard to undo! BOOM! It happens in a blink of an eye.

So, whatever your state of mind right now, Christmas will probably magnify it. If you're happy, you'll be happier, and if you're sad or lonely – well, you'll probably feel sadder or lonelier. What do you do with that? How do you rescue yourself from such a prediction? Like turning back the hands of time, it might feel impossible but there is something in this particular case that is 'doable'. For example, if on a scale of 1-10, you rate yourself as '2' in terms of loneliness. Don't focus on the loneliness or on 'not being lonely'. Instead, ask yourself 'how can I get to a 3 today?' Small achievable steps to feeling less lonely!

I've always struggled with complex emotions and memories – neither helped by being a complete empath. Bullying in secondary school along with a relentless bullying experience in a job I loved did not help things. No, I didn't choose it and 'why me?' often invades my mindscape. But I believe another person might not have survived it – such was its brutal-ness. So maybe that is the reason it was me. But without sounding like a 'cliché', it all led me to a more meaningful life! Akin to the 'monk that sold his Ferrari' – I did leave behind a convertible and more clothes than a boutique, to this life: fleeces, leggings and wellies!

I previously ran after a career in bright lights only to realise they can blind you to the cracks. Every stepping-stone, every choice (good and bad) has led me to here. No, it's not always a bed of roses! Like today, it was one of those days, when it's just you and the animals – who normally are enough of a buoyancy to keep me afloat on the toughest days, but today I knew I needed to have human company so I drove to a pretty town that had a beautiful cafe filled with cat photos and sat there enjoying just being 'in company' – maybe not in my company, but it was still company. So, that pushed me up the emotion ruler. I went from a 5 to a 6!

If you are sitting there in the 'why me' space, under the gaze of the magnifying glass of Christmas, start with getting out of the 'cul-de-sac'. Yes, physically walk away. Yes, feel the feelings, but walk with hope, find a purpose (small or big) to give yourself a break away from the over-thinking and try learn! The purpose can be from 'taking that walk you keep putting off' or 'ringing someone that needs that call' to whatever is purposeful. Then, keep learning what works and what doesn't work when that dark space sucks you in again. The fact is: lessons repeat themselves until we learn.

So, as I sit with the cats listening to 'Fairytale of New York', I too at times will find myself sitting under the magnifying glass of Christmas and in that 'why me' space. But the difference between this Christmas and many past Christmases is now I have a life purpose: rescuing and giving a sanctuary to as many neglected and abused animals that we can fit in. In fact, if I really became mindful and filled my head and heart with gratitude, I would realise they are my Christmas every day.

I once was a very reluctant rescuer – unable for the suffering of animals that crossed my path, so I had to rescue them to also ease my own pain probably. Today I'm just a rescuer – well, probably more a carer, along with Pat, of this pretty big rescue family here. I ask the 'why me?' less and just admit 'this is me!' And that's a better fit. Like swimming with the tide rather than against it.

Yes, the magnifying glass of Christmas will always make

the problems bigger than they are, and for me accentuate what is often a lonely place to be when you hold a dying animal or watch a horse limp out of a box half-starved, or wonder how you'll manage the next big vet bill and that is when you step out from under its glare and remind yourself, as my late mum used to: 'one day at a time'.

When the handle comes off the door

January 8th, 2021

You never are ready for the unwanted Christmas 'gifts' that are the adult version of the surprise you never asked for. The surprise you wish you could return to sender.

On Christmas Day the handle came off my door literally and not so literally. As I closed the front door the handle came off in my hands with ease. Christmas Day was the day when I came undone. Nothing stops the ravelling that begins within. But when you get a grip on the panic and get really grounded – it's really amazing how the perceived personal mess moves away like grey clouds in a potential blue sky. The clouds are still there lurking, but you have got respite to breathe deeply and fish for a solution rather than feeling thrown overboard. Solutions end most problems after all. Why can't we remember that when we need to most? I am conscious that there are some life's certainties that no solution can remedy.

So, my Christmas became my end and my beginning all at once. One part still clinging to the idea of 'it will be OK' comforted me. My rescue life has constantly lifted these words like a weight to build up necessary muscle. And during these times we need lots of mental muscle that leads to resilience.

Time alone does not come up with solutions. You could be waiting forever. And as I continue this post now where I left off, it's a week into January and rationality, dialogue, and lots of YouTube mediations and Ted Talks later – all is OK. Yes, different, but OK. You manage the hurt by getting on with life as best you can and loving yourself and those you love more. When you care for so many animals who have not had the best start in life, you face many endings. One replaces the other but suddenly all the endings can hit you at once: every person you have lost, every animal that has died in your arms, it becomes a collective loss and you feel their 'goneness' all at once. At the moment a little rescue cat is fighting to stay alive, fighting a virus that has invaded her body and took away the power of her legs. She has a fighting chance. But it is up to her now. The vets have played their part. Her name is Star: in name and in nature. She is the tiny kitten a man rescued from between pallets, and the vet said she might not survive – that was over a year ago.

It's 3:30am and I'm eating stew. No, not my first choice of food at this 'should be in bed' time, but it's the sudden realisation of the need for self-care to be able to other-care and to give my body nutrients I have literally starved myself of.

I haven't slept for more than 3 block hours since December the 22nd. Sugar is my substitute for sleep. Star needs intensive care and my greatest fear is one of our rescues dying alone. It has happened and it's desperately sad. They survived way too long on their own before getting here; I try so hard to ensure they don't leave us on their own. I'm typing this and reading hard to digest medical articles and other on-line resources about boosting a cat's immunity, and at the same time being sold cures from the black market used by many vets in China.

Pat has been busy feeding starving horses and pulling some out of rivers. He really is a hero to so many horses and to me! One wealthy landowner made it known today that he doesn't want hungry horses fed on his land. He owns the land but not the horses. He finished the conversation by saying 'I'm an animal lover!'

Ireland's chronic equine crisis is really an ugly truth we are not acknowledging. The suffering is unimaginable. Imagine being a pregnant mare stuck in a river overnight in freezing temperatures. Imagine she was driven in by thrill seekers on quads. Imagine she was skeletal. I look at our rescue ponies, and I'm so grateful we got them out of these types of cruel situations.

I try to spend lots of time with the Croga Collies. With them I'm reminded of where bravery takes you: it only takes you forward. So, I'm boosting my bravery again for 2021 by holding on tight to those words of simple, but powerful solace, 'it will be OK' lifting and lifting, them up and up, again and again. If I'm not brave, I can't be brave for the animals that come here.

As I finish my stew, I'm thinking I'd prefer Weetabix with warm milk and there is a time and place for stew. Just like there is a time to worry and a time to take a break from it. I'm going to have a 'worry o'clock' in 2021 – when I sit down and face all the worries I had during the day but refused entry to. Worry and stress really should have a time and place. It's pointless saying 'don't worry' – maybe we should say 'worry later!' during its allocated time.

I found it hard to come up with a title for this book. I thought 'letting love in' was appropriate as the rescue animals here show me how they are so brave to let love in again after being failed by so many. But it was my brother, Frank, who suggested this title, 'loving the loveless'. So many animals in this world are loveless. Rescue work may be difficult and complex at times but loving these animals is the easy part. Loving them – the loveless, teaches us so much about love and about ourselves.

True love is indeed unconditional; it is without limitations; it is without conditions. This is how animals love us.

If everyday was one little life

February, 2021

Some people would say we really are just a number of days. So everyday should be like one little life – if we are to get the best out of our days here. What should go into these days if money could not dictate its amazingness? Could we make our days more meaningful and more memorable if they were devoid of the 'all that glitters is gold' ideas of happiness – those 'if I won the lotto' scenarios. I have a feeling – like love – we might be looking for happiness in all the wrong places when money makes up our sign posts. Yes, it's essential for essentials and not having it makes each day like a lifetime. But should enough be simply enough. Without a lot of it, don't we become more reliant on the simpler things? And right now your best memories are probably ones that didn't cost a penny.

There was a time money was really important to me; it became a constant life goal: to be rich! It even became an attractive characteristic- if someone had money, I tended to have more of an interest in them. But, big cars and lots of cash never made up for bad traits. I surprised myself one day when a boyfriend at the time (a well-known musician) forgot my birthday and literally flung his credit card at me when he finally got my obvious hints. 'Buy what you want,' he grumpily said. My birthday surprise was, I cried, and suddenly I didn't just see him for what he was, because I probably always knew but blocked it, but I saw him as someone I didn't want to be with. Yes, I was sad and what a gift that was: to not be so blinded anymore and to be aware of what I did need. This incident came soon after another 'enlightening moment' when he was driving me to college in a car that turned heads, I spotted a friend of mine getting a lift on the bar of her boyfriend's bike and I was jealous. Jealous of how happy they looked. And I was miserable. Part of me still thought I could grow immune to the miserableness. How blessed am I that I didn't. From where I'm looking now – my life is priceless-watching our rescue donkey trying to keep up with two rescued hyper ponies. Hay is my gold and if they are healthy and happy, I am too.

Today I read a post how people are investing in metal collars/leads for their dogs so dog-nappers can't use bolt cutters to steal dogs. Yes, we are now experiencing a moral pandemic: what is priceless to you has become a price tag to someone else. You could even get shot or stabbed if you don't release your pet to these people. As happened Lady Gaga's dog walker: shot multiple times as he wouldn't hand over her dogs. It's telling: more pets being stolen, more people cashing in on the 'Covid-buck' by selling their own pets, and microchips being dug out with blades from the backs of stolen pets. And whilst this is about animals, I want to be mindful about the increase in calls to domestic abuse organisations and to ChildLine. Yes, something is broken when so many people are not just no longer happy in their homes, they are no longer safe. Till death do us part becomes a desperately sad wish rather than a vow.

Today was a sad day here as some of the ponies who are part of the 'Hay not Roses' feeding initiative were taken away from their herd by their owner. We asked where they were being taken to but there was no exact location given. There never is. One of them is a tiny tot who was very well minded by the herd. He would whinny and run back and forth from them to us, to let them know we had arrived. Another one is a frail filly foal who is so very close to her mother. Pat tried to reason with them that she could do with staying a bit longer as we were trying to build her up. The reply, 'she's grand!' She isn't and she won't be unless she gets lots of care. But it's all about the money and how many horses you have for some people. Why aren't a few horses enough? Why do you need to fill fields with as many horses as possible? Nobody needs so many horses – like clothes hanging in wardrobes you never wear and you forget about. These are forgotten horses until a sale comes along or a 'swap'. Yes, the dreaded swap! 'Anyone got anything to swap for this….' And you look at the photo of another foal whose eyes try reach through the lens to get a message to someone somewhere 'help me, I am worth more than a packet of cigarettes or a raffle ticket!' And then there are the sellers, who take their family pony from a lovely paddock and stable and sell him/her into a world they cannot cope with! Sure, the kids are gone to college or have outgrown her/him. They weren't born into the hard life but the need to make a few quid buys them a forgotten horse label. How can people be so calculated and cruel? Why don't you want to know where your pony has gone? Or is the person who pulled your pony from you at the fair enough to tell you what is to come for your family pet?

People give out about 'nanny states' – but from what I see – life is beautiful but a lot of people in this world have become extremely cruel and that is worse than this Covid pandemic. It will probably kill more people and test so many more. We need minding. A lot of minding. And we need to be mindful – not a mind full of things and thoughts that contribute nothing to your 'real happiness' or to others who share your life space.

I can only speak for myself but there is enough evidence in my life story alone to prove that 'money definitely does not buy happiness'. I have never had so little but I've never been so happy. Here, at Hilltop, we all have enough and with that 'enough' fulfilled we don't have to waste our energy on wanting more or needing more. We just keep it in the day…. one day at a time because tomorrow is not guaranteed for any of us.

It is so important to mind yourself so you can mind everything else and everyone else you share your world with.

The Sometimes Fixable Fate

March 24th, 2021

Yesterday we lost a little rescue called Ashling: a calico who did automatic flips to get a belly rub as you passed. She personified sweetness. Losing a rescue plunges your mind back into the 'what ifs' and they can torture us. Our minds, if given a choice, would choose worry and stress as a default setting. I guess that's why working on peace of mind is one of the most difficult and never-ending tasks. Sometimes it's nearly easier to admit defeat and return to what we know best: worrying. But here's the thing about rescuing & working with animals – 'the thing' that reenforces what was taught and practiced way before book shops had a wellness section: distraction, practicalities and purpose plugs that hole you would could sink into and forces you back out into the world and out of your own mind. We all need to be aware of what is 'really going on for us' and to look at our thoughts and feelings but to stay in our own heads all of the time is not healthy.

As Ashling passed, another little rescue appeared: not even a year old and pregnant. I often think do some rescues let go knowing another is waiting for a space. And now the tears have started as I give myself these moments to just sit with my sadness.

This 'chair' will be kicked from under me in a minute by 'time to get going again'. It's important to feel the feelings but it's more important to manage their potential to take over you. It's like breaking a leg, crutches help you continue, and in my case here: purpose.

Here, at Hilltop Sanctuary, thinking about animal cruelty and dealing with it, can really overwhelm me sometimes, and I find myself in tears working my way around the yard. Again, it is good to feel the feelings, but to take a break from them too – keep shifting the gear so we don't get stuck.

Reframing in rescue is nearly perfected without us realising it. A horse arrives in with all the hallmarks of extreme cruelty and a passer-by might comment 'what the hell is wrong with people?' whilst the rescuer might quickly add 'sure it's great she gets a new start'. Both looking at the same broken horse but both with different frames to put around him. Reframing gives immediate hope and often necessary blocking.

Ashling should never have been born to live in a burnt-out car with her mommy and her sisters. That wasn't her fate. Someone decided it when they didn't spay her mum. Her mum was not feral so someone somewhere did handle her at some stage. A Woman/Man could have created another fate. Ashling has died but she should never have been born.

When my mother passed away, I always remember what a lovely nun wrote in a card to us following her death: Anne got well. At the time in my anger and upset, I failed to see her kind reasoning of what was a tragedy for us. In death, she will never suffer again and did get well. She suffered terribly a year prior to her passing.

Ashling was loved so much whilst here and as she drew her last breaths, I prayed, that her passing would not be painful. It wasn't. Our new rescue is named Starling in memory of Star (who passed a few months ago) and Ashling.

At the moment I could say fate has cast a cloud on the sanctuary with recent challenging news we have received, but I guess that would be defeatist if we just give up, so we are going to try intervene before anyone might console me with the words 'sure, everything for a reason' or 'that's your fate!' And I do get those sayings and expressions as they can help you move to that lovely space of acceptance – whether it's forever or short-lived – the latter at least gives you respite.

Life is certainly complex – but life is akin to the cake you take out of the oven: it just might be perfect because you followed the step by step recipe, or it might be a disaster even after you follow the recipe. The difference is: how you react to each scenario. With gratitude or in the last case, 'sure, I'll just try again another time!'

Fixable fate…. no harm in trying again and again as the alternative is 'no cake' ever.

Let me tell you about vile

May 3rd, 2021

Anger seemed to follow me around the yard yesterday – like a shadow I couldn't separate from. And behind that blinding emotion lied a lot of other more understandable ones, that I looked at during the night as I bottle fed a new-born kitten.

On Sunday I read the word 'vile' and 'scum' many times as it reappeared on retweets and comments and in on-line discussions. In between these popular and over-shared posts, the other vileness I'm used to popped its tragic head up as if to remind me 'I'm still here!'. Will the real Vileness, please stand up? And it did. There is a lot of cruelty we deal with that we can't share. So, one word with the same rigid meaning but misused/misplaced in one story: the one that wasn't only stealing the vileness spotlight but taking a word I'm used to and applying it to an experience that seemed so far removed from vile. Maybe words like 'disappointing' or 'inappropriate' might have suited the 'hurt' party better. And they did seem angry! What was really going on is only known to them? And yes, how can you not feel sorry that they see things in a way they don't have to.

And then I watched how so many people became consumed with this story and gave their time, their energy to what should have been a 'back and forth' conversation between one well-known presenter and a journalist. I don't know, maybe I felt the word belonged to others: those who deal with the uglier side to life, those who try to remedy it, and maybe the real owners of such an ugly word belongs to those who actually live in 'vileness' every minute of every day.

And then I thought about what do we get from certain spreads – like a six-page-spread of a heavily pregnant presenter in her underwear or in a bathtub. How does it add to our day or our lives? Is it something we aspire to: to be photographed nearly naked for the some of the world to see? Whose life are we feeding?

I know this sounds absurd but I wish some journalist rang me up or emailed me to ask me the name of the kitten I was bottle feeding to highlight the real vileness of a world where unwanted kittens are born to unneutered cats and left to suffer so much. Thousands of kittens right now are lying on wet ground as the rain pours down, their mommies have gone to find food or maybe gone elsewhere – maybe she is too young to feed them or has no milk. Mice and rats will circle them and for a moment these new-borns with their eyes shut tight mistake them for their mommy. Yes, it is vile and I even hate the reader of this to have to see these words. A baby is a baby: two legs or four! I don't think I'm much different from you or anyone but what feeds the soul and the mind is 'doing good' – intervening in vileness. It changes not just our lives but saves lives. And yes, we can have that balance: dipping into the escapism of glitz and glamour and that celebrity gossip but maintaining that purpose to want to make a difference. There is too much vileness out there for what feels like a 'handful' of people to deal with. If there was a recruitment campaign – it could last forever as cruelty is on-going and constant: it's like a fire that will never go out, but the damage can be minimised by proactive extinguishing compassion.

My heart went out to Niamh Walsh yesterday. I didn't know she covered entertainment. I only know her as a journalist dedicated to highlighting animal cruelty and puppy farms. I know on a smaller scale what it is like to be on the receiving end of someone's unwarranted wrath. I've had to threaten legal action on two rescuers (yes, who would believe?) who really were determined to push me to the edge and one nearly did. One was angry I searched for a dog they lost: she didn't want anyone to look for the dog or it be known they lost a dog who they rescued from a yard where he lived with an embedded collar tied in a ditch. It took two days of walking fields and setting traps, but we got him and brought him to the home that was home checked for him. She put it on social media platforms that I stole a rescue dog when I searched for a rescue dog she didn't want found. The second rescuer simply didn't like me and wanted to destroy my name. So, it happens everywhere: some people don't mind their own issues so they take them out (undeservedly) on someone else.

Niamh Walsh wasn't hiding in a ditch with a long lens; she did nothing different than any other entertainment journalist requesting information. I can't see this presenter ever calling any of the more well-known names in the journalism industry 'vile'. And it's a great pity she threw that word at a journalist who exposes so much vileness. The puppy farm industry personifies the word.

Back to Starling's last kitten who passed away during the night. I can't express the complete heartbreak when you make a bottle, put a heat-pad in the microwave and make your way to feed a baby, just a few days old. You can't wait to see them, to see how they are, and you go on your knees to look into the crib, and you search for a breath and instead you find stillness, and you look at the warm bottle that you had for them. You look at his mommy who is confused and goes between 'I need to go now' to 'running back in to be with him!' Mixed emotions and reactions from a mommy who is a kitten herself. I had moved them to the main house on the yard as I felt the barking from the senior rescue room/yard was too much for them so I put them in a room upstairs in Pat's house. It was quieter but below them they could hear all the comings and goings. Last night I put Starling in a carrier and put her last baby on the heat pad and put a little blanket over him. And we walked in the dark back to the cabin/catio where her journey began here as a young pregnant cat. It was a surreal walk in the dark – leaving behind a tiny soul but it would have been beyond cruel to leave her there all night with her baby. She is a different cat this morning: angry, hissing, unsure of her world now.

So, I guess my point is this: Starling is not feral. She is someone's cat and they didn't neuter her and for a moment I'm going to be selfish and say this: you passed this on to me, nights of no sleep, other rescues neglected , bottle feeding kittens, trying to keep them alive, dealing with a grieving mother. You, who failed your cat, passed this on to me and set this beautiful little cat up to suffer. And yes, when done intentionally, it is vile.

Here's to Starling and her babies. She was the best mother who wasn't ready to be one, and they adored her.

The Ugly Story about a Duckling

May 12th, 2021

When I was eleven, I asked Alan Deegan who was in my class to carve our names in a heart up high on a tree. Now I was so in love (in the eleven year old sense) that I thought 'sure why wouldn't we have our names carved on a tree' that happened to stand like a leafy tower in a well-maintained hedge that separated the national school and the church. Back then (pre 'stop & search' & knife crime) boys in the country tended to have pen-knifes and so Alan, probably afraid to say no, climbed that tree, and etched our names together and forever. Well, that was the plan!

The next day I was wondering what the commotion was around 'our tree' until I saw some of the first class had drawn the principal's attention to our names. Tell Tales!! Well, both myself and Alan were about to be 'beheaded' in an age-appropriate way. First off, the school ladder was brought out and I was instructed to hold it as Alan made his way to the top. And all the school were brought out to witness the undoing of the love etch. Yes, he had to scrape our names out of the tree. (Can you imagine an eleven-year-old climbing a ladder today in school?) Then we had to go to every class and tell them how we should not have done that. (My poor younger brother!) And finally, Father Gilmartin was called in by the school. Yes, maybe a bit of an over-reaction! We were given a talking to by a priest who put the fear of God in God himself! But, to this day I don't like anything etched into a tree or hammered – even those cute fairy doors. Why? Because whilst the principal might have over-reacted in the way he went about teaching us a lesson: it worked. I have a great respect for trees. Poor Alan, he barely managed all the attention. He was one of those boys whose cheeks went fiery red if you looked at him. I found it so lovely but he probably was ashamed of it. We never spoke after that day! I found a respect for trees but lost my national school Prince Charming to a shared silence.

The recent theft and selling of ducklings evoked diverse emotions and responses. There were the rational voices: 'Cop-on if you are a parent of one of these kids!' to 'Sure they wouldn't survive long anyway with their mothers!' to 'These boys are future serial killers!' to 'They are victims themselves of 'nothing to do'. (Rolling eyes!)

So, let's lay it out there and see can we figure out why in one case, a group of boys would steal ducklings away from very upset mother ducks and get on their bikes and whizz them through city traffic believing they would be famous with the video clip they were about to up-load! To add to the story, can we figure out why a group of boys would use their bikes to trip up women running for a train or to push one onto a line. The 'figuring out part' can tie you in knots of explanations and then throw you into a mental maze of disillusionment with life, where the only relief comes from those irrational thoughts of 'that's it, I'm moving to the Aran Islands'.

I recall writing an article on unprovoked attacks on the streets of Galway City. Interviewing young men who had jumped up and down on someone's head (who agreed to be interviewed) was both stomach churning and insightful. The answers would start with 'I dunno why I did it…' to letting me in on tactics, 'We would say the fifth lad with black hair would get it, to 'They were weird anyway!' Always find the 'weird' and 'freak' justifications interesting when one would question how weird is the act of intentionally setting out to hurt someone who you don't know. The current Cornation Street story-line – based on the real-life death of Sophia Lancaster: a sweet and smart young woman who was engaged in a conversation by a group of young people who decided to kill her because she was 'weird' in their eyes, is a poignant reminder of how young people justify bullying, violence and even death. Weird being: she read a lot of books and didn't do typical street wear but liked to be different. Oh yes, different! Why do some people have an emotional explosive reaction to difference?

Anyway, back to the theft of baby ducklings and the boys with the bikes and on the bikes. You see, each of us have dealt with some sort of issue/issues as children, as teenagers, as adults but how many of us have taken the turmoil or hurt we felt and loaded it up to project it on to an innocent person or animal? How many of us have experienced complete boredom and gone out and knelt by the canal and shoved ducklings into our pockets or threw a lady under a train? Anger, hurt, frustration or boredom doesn't explain these events. Choice does (unless there is a cognitive disability)! Every minute of every day we choose how to react, and yes, we often have knee-jerk reactions that might not always be justified but most of the time we go 'sorry about that!' SORRY! Another key word. Without remorse more ducklings will be stolen to die terrible deaths and more people will be victims of unprovoked attacks.   How do we deal with the negative choices young people make? Is it too late? Not if you're facing a toddler today who screams and screams and you can manage to delay gratification for his/her demand or even introduce the word 'NO' in a positive sense and show them 'it's not the end of the world' word. 'No' often means, 'I care enough about you to not give into every demand'. You see if we introduce 'No' in nice ways like 'Maybe another day' or 'Not for now' or 'We'll see' at a young age – the bigger 'NOs' will be more digestible as they get older. So, maybe if your son/daughter doesn't get their way with a person who prefers not to have sex, they can manage 'No', and say 'sorry, I understand!' rather than sexually assaulting that person, or maybe when they hear the word 'No, I don't want you mixing with people doing drugs/dealing drugs,' or 'No, a duckling does not belong in this house and no, you won't sell him for five euros!' They'll digest the 'No' with ease as they have had plenty of practice as children

The truth is: guardians and parents are now afraid to say 'No' and it is that word deficiency in the family home's vocabulary that has probably contributed to a lot of cruelty to animals and people. There is an insatiable, selfish, need gratification that develops that doesn't do 'No' and it's very ugly. It's akin to a horror vacuum where no morals, empathy or compassion can grow. Attempts are made to fill it with activities and acts that don't sit well with most of us. Yes, there are exceptions. I know of parents/guardians who did everything right and things still went belly-up!

So, I guess this is where consequences come in: those implemented by bodies outside of the family home. When we tell the world that we won't control our behaviour, that responsibility has to be handed over to someone outside of you. After all when young people choose to act illegally or cruelly, well there has to be consequences but not just with fines, or ASBOs, or time in a juvenile detention centre: there has to be some other remedy, one that helps intervene in this 'choice behaviour'. Like the boy in Dublin who tortured a hedgehog and served no time. Why wasn't he instructed under supervision to work with an animal charity for a number of hours. Empathy can be grown but not in a dark needy vacuum with no interventions. We have to intervene urgently with what exists in these vacuums of 'I can do what I want because….' The 'becauses' don't actually matter because we are all products of 'becauses', and they might explain our emotional scars but will never excuse 'scarring' another because of them. I've come face to face with boys/young men cruel to animals and let me tell you, whilst my heart raced, and my head said 'run' – my heart stayed for the animal. And no, it doesn't always work in your favour. But one time it worked. A pony was being beaten to move, by a few young lads. I happened to be there feeding as the horses/ponies here were eating weeds, bark, moss. So, I grabbed a bucket of hard feed and handed it to one of the boys. I got the usual 'she doesn't know what a bucket is or hard feed' lines and yes, they were right, but I said, 'well, she is going to know now!' I got him to give her some of the nuts from the bucket first and then got him to shake the bucket and walk ahead and the pony started to walk. I saw a glimpse of pride in that boy's eyes and of course I left without my bucket and a bag of feed as they all wanted to try it with the other ponies. With a warning they would kill them with too much feed, one boy was put in charge of that. So that bucket and hard feed gave those boys another choice: not to just hit her to move but to shake a bucket. I'm aware that their old ways might always pull stronger but at least they were shown 'another way!' Three years later, last Christmas that passed, I was invited into a national school as a boy had something to give the sanctuary. I was given a drawing of a horse and twenty-five euros donation. The boy who handed it to me was one of those boys.

The Ugly Duckling (the story) has a lot to teach us about not judging people by how they look and being happy with ourselves. The last few days has taught us more: there is nothing ugly about ducklings. There is simply too much ugly behaviour out there.

I learnt at eleven, we can't just go around and mark our names on beautiful trees, and the consequence of doing so thought me that valuable lesson. Meaningful lessons we learn as children often do last a lifetime. Like a meandering river they mould and shape us. Lessons in empathy and respect from an early age help young people grow into adults who love and respect themselves; they will have no need to harm another human being or inflict suffering on an animal as a way to deal with their own inner hate.

Loving the loveless, whether human or animal, is the kindest gift we can give another. It is an extraordinary gift that gives twice: to both the giver and to the recipient.

Nowzad: the life lesson in a word

September 1st, 2021

If you have an innate love and respect for all lives, the last few days as Afghanistan became undone was akin to that desperately sad movie that you hope is not based on a true story. But the irony is art constantly copies life and in the strangest and cruellest of fiction lies someone's truths and life story. Yes, movies will be made about the last week in Kabul and the race to evacuate people, but these future movies will be based on the real-life horror that is unfolding in our now. Afghanistan may be far removed from us geographically but the sight of babies sacrificed by parents over barbed wire so they will know a life free of fear, or live feeds from Nowzad pleading for help to get staff and rescues out brought them all into our hearts, minds (well, most of us!) and our nows!

I guess for the purpose of this post, I'm going to focus on the Nowzad rescues and their rescuers. The last few days of wondering would they or wouldn't they get out, and watching some of the media debates and discussions formed by political and public reaction, hit the 'on button' for that illuminating lens through which we view what man is really made of. And some of it for the animal lover was pretty ugly and difficult to digest. It showed us how there is a cohort that like to poke that simmering fire of animals versus people and in doing so a rigid line appears and you pick your side. Even though there was never a case of rescues taking the place of people on planes, there were so many that wanted to hold on to 'they will' like a soother to sooth the seemingly irritating dislike of animals and those people like Pen Farthing who probably would have risked his life for them. People like Pen bring up so much for people that are very unlike him and instead of gently looking at that, a venomous reaction often forms and 'what's really going on?' never gets answered. And so, the hate game continues.

I've come across this hate – often disguised in a suspiciously sneery or snobbish guise when you cross paths with those people who look at you like you are mad to care so much. As a fanatical (because sometimes you have to be in a world that does not deserve animals) animal lover, advocate, rescuer, some people say it without saying it, 'what the hell is wrong with you?' But it's like pointing that finger of blame – yes, the finger might be perfectly placed in the right direction (sometimes) but a lot of the time it's the direction of the other three fingers that tell us more! Does the blame lie with the finger pointer?

I wonder do people who love deeply irritate those who love superficially. Do people who care so much niggle at the parts in others who care so little. Is it jealousy or is it total suspicion or maybe it is hate but the hate probably grows from the other uncomfortable emotional seedlings. So, what if we dug deeper without this turning into a paper on human behaviour.

What about our core beliefs? Yes, the personal petrol that pretty much forms us. Core beliefs are a person's most central ideas about themselves, others, and the world. These beliefs act like a lens through which every situation and life experience is seen. Because of this, people with different core beliefs might be in the same situation, but think, feel, and behave very differently. And that to excuse the pun, is the core of the issue, in many disputes, or in this case, the Defence Secretary's reaction to Pen Farthing and his 'pets' to quote Mr.Wallace. He could not get around the concept of rescues or maybe he did but chose to poke Mr.Farthing and his followers by using the wrong term – Which also is telling about his CBs. Both men seeing the same situation – albeit, one in the situation but seeing it very differently.

Our core beliefs are formed over time depending on our life experiences. The good thing is: negative, irrational or wrong core beliefs can be changed. But they weren't going to change quick enough to get the Nowzad rescue team and their animals out so the evacuation was planned and attempted by themselves as they navigated a difficult journey to Kabul airport whilst they dealt with another enemy from afar: the media and officialdom back home.

There is a saying that says, 'those who never love an animal, part of their soul remains untouched!' and that was apparent as I watched many television debates and read many articles about Operation Ark. Noah never would have saved breeding pairs if social media existed: he would have probably given up with the realisation, 'what kind of a f@@ked up world am I saving them for?'

Some people just don't get it as their souls remain untouched. They know not of the unconditional love of an animal or being loving by a pet who loves them more than they actually love themselves so they go through life seeking it – often from the wrong people and in all the wrong places.

I probably overuse the question, 'what's really going on?' when people are reacting in a way that doesn't quite fit with what is happening. And to change core beliefs requires a heap load of honesty and catching yourself when you resort to the old beliefs that serve no purpose, are defunct, or they form a mind that tries to demean or damage those who don't represent your own beliefs.

Nowzad means new, to begin again. And that is a forever word that reminds us why animals matter too; why it's never about animals versus people; and the importance of animals to many people – whether they are pets or their only family member. There is no argument needed and the debate is futile. Animals would tell us so if they could. We could learn so much from them if only our beliefs would allow the lesson in.

It is not over for Nowzad as their founder is determined to complete Operation Ark and save his staff who are 'terrified' as they live in a very dangerous world now – some of them were not even born into. It is alien to them. To quote one Afghan woman, 'it is like being in an abusive relationship.'

It's important to be mindful that both people and animals will suffer under the Taliban. I will be praying for both.

When a live line becomes a noose

September 12th, 2021

You have to admire any presenter whose show runs like a conducted orchestra. Joe's leading questions, on Live line, are like those hands dancing in the air to the sounds they are extracting. The hands that knows the sound before the musician has delivered it. Joe can certainly play people very well. Their drawn-out answers are exactly the way he wants the show to go. It just goes down the wrong path sometimes and when it comes to suffering – the comedy path is distasteful and regretful.

Certain topics shouldn't be messed with by injecting humour or shock jock OMGs exaggerated words and breaths (Philip Boucher Hayes, filling in for Joe one day, deserves an Oscar for) into. Topics involving suffering should be researched and empathy should be the hand directing the information shared so no more harm should happen to, in this case, feral cats. Otherwise the narrative of 'sure, it's only a cat!' gets spoon fed into the open mouths of those who love to say, 'I told you so!' so they can continue to lay poison, continue to dump them, and continue to hate. In the minds of those who 'I don't know if I like cats,' the veiled hate campaign might just win them over. Does hate make better radio? Apparently so.

If we were to refer to Liveline this week, to determine who is to blame for our country's woes, one would say 'feral cats'. Afterall, one did kill Gerry's fish and he of course decided the best way to deal with his problem and loss was to move the 'problem' on. Clever Gerry sacrificed a wheelie bin to make the perfect trap to catch the cat. No, he didn't take him or her to the vet to check for a chip, or he didn't put up a notice locally to see did anyone own the cat. Afterall, some of us (God forbid) actually own and love, wait for it…Feral Cats! Good old Gerry drove the poor trapped cat far away from his territory, his home, and dumped him. Did you know cats are more connected to their territory than their people? Not by choice, but by survival. And then there was Catherine who recorded her newly adopted 'psycho cat' sounding so stressed as he tried to make sense of his new home. He was crying because he was afraid. A lot of us cry when really afraid or if we miss where we came from-like all other sentient beings. But Oh, No! He was called PSYCHO and Joe kept playing the sound bite – well, for entertainment of course! Silly me! Now if this was a puppy or a child crying in terror, we would have been all clambering to get on Liveline to express our disgust and upset that they were being laughed at. But not quite so, because it now seems not many of us have a problem with feral cats suffering. And that is the crux of the issue: why hundreds of colonies exist in Ireland and also explains all the solitary little cats that just go around in circles in their territory – maybe afraid to join a colony or not accepted by any or hoping some human might keep the hunger at bay for another day. A lot of people justify their suffering, not just by not liking them, but by hating them.

Nine out of ten hunts fail for cats so can you imagine being weak from hunger and further exhausted by hunting? Now imagine being heavily pregnant. I accept some people genuinely don't like cats (phobia reasons) but as a staff member said to me in Tesco's one day as she scanned my 40th tin of sardines in sunflower oil, 'I don't like cats, but I would never want them to suffer so I feed a feral cat behind the shop!'

Before I finish, I want to end with the lady who began her moment of airtime with the line, 'feral cats can harm people too'. Or maybe she said 'kill'…anyway, her daughter got a tick off a feral cat. Now, there was no concrete proof of this but given the directed narrative, sure It's best to be conclusive, and keep in with the argument created: feral cats are bad bad bad. They kill fish, cry when afraid, and there's just too many of them, for God's (Joe's, Philip's) sake!!!!! Yes, feral cats are now to blame for ticks too. Never mind all the other animals we find them on or the grass we walk in.

Liveline did no favours to feral cats this week. Feral because they are without a home. Feral because someone somewhere did not neuter their pet cat. Feral is not a title, is not a feared ugly word. Feral is the way they exist to survive. Feral is their fear. Feral is a real struggle. Feral is our problem because we, yes us humans, we created it! And Joe, that is no joke!

Thank you for reading loving the loveless . . .

Printed in Great Britain
by Amazon

85062132R00132